Baker & Spice

exceptional breads

Dan Lepard &
Richard Whittington

Quadrille

Publishing director Jane O'Shea
Creative director Helen Lewis
Project editor Janet Illsley
Art director Mary Evans
Food for photography Dan Lepard
Stylist Róisín Nield
Design Paul Welti
Production Bridget Fish

First published in 2007 by
Quadrille Publishing Limited
Alhambra House
27-31 Charing Cross Road
London WC2H 0LS
www.quadrille.co.uk

Text © 1999 Richard Whittington and Dan
Lepard

Recipe photography © 1999 Peter Williams

Location photography © 1999 Emily Andersen

Design and layout © 2007 Quadrille Publishing
Limited

Cataloguing in Publication Data:
a catalogue record for this book is available
from the British Library

ISBN-13: 978 1 84400 4515

Printed in China

Contents

Introduction 6

Essentials 14

Handling bread doughs 30

Shaping loaves 44

Shaping rolls 50

Baking with wild yeasts 56

Wild yeast starters 62

Wild yeast breads 72

Baking with commercial yeast 88

Flat breads and shaped doughs 114

Sweet yeast breads 130

Quick breads 146

Glossary 154

Index 156

Acknowledgements 160

"I think bread is special, something simple and honest yet delicious. Every time you break it, smell it, eat it, it makes life a little better, even if it is only for 5 minutes. Good bread is something you never get bored with. It delights afresh, every day. In essence, it describes both who we are at Baker & Spice and why we are." GAIL STEPHENS

Introduction

BAKER & SPICE'S original shop that once sat so prettily in London's smart Walton Street started its life as a window for Gail Stephens' existing trade-baking business. It was only gradually, as the Victorian ovens were restarted and on-site production began for the local community, that it took shape and flourished, developing the unique identity that has made it famous. Other shops have since opened, in Belgravia, Queen's Park and Maida Vale.

With a cult following across London and beyond, Baker & Spice is the most successful boutique-style food retailer in the country. When you visit the shops, first impressions are overwhelming. This is the bakery and pâtissierie of your dreams and those dreams were probably set in Paris, not London. As you admire the stacks of beautiful breads and trays of captivating pastries giving off their sweet, alluring smells – all of them hand-made by bakers working on the premises and using traditional ingredients and methods – it is hard to believe that the roots of such excellence were in vans, not stone ovens, in a delivery service for bread baked by other people, for customers too small for the big bakers to be bothered with. Today's shining star in British artisanal baking has its roots in an innovative and successful service operation. A sound business administration providing financial independence allowed Gail Stephens to set the shop up in a way that was thought by many to be commercially untenable in today's marketplace.

"The way the shop is run is really based on how we trade," she says, explaining that the raw ingredients define an attitude as well as a style of food. "I have always been concerned about the provenance as well as the quality of the ingredients we work with. I have never bought solely on price and was warned that my ethical concerns would bankrupt me. The irony is that today the business is very successful."

"We are what we buy, and that has moral as well as price consequences. We use as much that is organic as possible. We work with the seasons and are very careful about where our raw materials come from. Does it have to travel half way round the world to get here? If something comes from the Third World, who exploited whom to get it here? I don't sit in the office and buy blind on the telephone. I go to Covent Garden market daily, and read and check every label on every box of fresh produce that I buy. I smell and feel the goods as well as taste them. Once a month I go to a big dried fruit, nut and spice importer. Buying is never on auto-pilot. I really spend a lot of time with suppliers to get it right."

"Everything we sell is baked on the premises. What you see is what you get and what you get is what we make. And that involves

learned technique and very hard work. The point of Baker & Spice is that it is self-contained; we don't buy in anything ready-made. We do things the way people used to do them, which in the age of factory farming and supermarkets have largely been forgotten." Practically, that means seven 18-hour working days in every week.

"Changes occur in what is baked in some sense by natural progression, but also by listening to the customers. Partly because of that we have become a real village shop. We are the neighbourhood. We reflect it and it reflects us."

Baker & Spice is remarkable in its consistency, which is the direct consequence of the calibre of the staff. Those who work here are part of a team and they share the same commitment to quality, achieved in an ethical environment. It is not like a restaurant where front of house and back of house function autonomously, often with a degree of animosity. Here the two are clearly, happily and inextricably intertwined. They work together and you cannot see the join because the service is a seamless process from the cooking to the customer. Those who cook at the back often communicate with the customers, sometimes even serving them. As freshly baked loaves are brought through, they are discussed and commented on. "The shop has to work from the front to the back and from the back to the front. It is important that the people who cook the food don't feel separated from the selling of it. They come in and out of the shop and they talk to the customers. This is exactly how we all feel it should be."

THE BAKERY

Underneath the street level in Walton Street are two brick ovens, each with the original stone-covered baking floor covering 10 square metres. They were built and installed in 1902. Originally fuelled by coal, the steam-generating ovens also provided hot water for the bakery. The steam in a professional oven helps to develop the crust and gives a wonderful bronze colour to the bread.

During the 1950s, the ovens were oil-fired, the fuel being piped from outside tanks to the burners that ran around the oven. The smoke and excess steam were carried through a twisting tunnel to escape from the chimney, so contributing to the smogs that polluted London's air until the Clean Air Act was introduced in 1957.

When Gail Stephens took over the property from Justin de Blank these ovens were still in use, by then fired by gas. After minor renovations and the addition of a steam-injection system, the ovens were ready to bake bread once again.

Traditionally, breads are put into the oven on heavily floured wooden peels – flat beechwood heads attached to long shafts – imported from France. Another investment was a double-sized *parisienne*, a cupboard used to protect the dough as it rests on unbleached linen sheets. Dozens of cloth-lined reed baskets, in which the big sourdoughs sit during their long fermentation, help to shape the loaves as they prove, again sourced from France. For breads that

require a long, chilled rest over many hours, a temperature-controlled retarder-prover that could hold over 200 small loaves was installed.

Another introduction was an Artofex mixer, a British machine invented to replicate the hand-kneading of doughs in wooden troughs, which was the standard practice in bakeries for hundreds of years. Its unique configuration helps give the bread an irregular aeration – different sized bubbles of air throughout the crumb – and its gentle slow mixing helps develop the gluten strands.

THE BREADS

Similar constructions of flour, water and yeast can deliver very different textures and complex, deep flavours. Wheat flours, from the darkest moist wholewheat to cream-coloured, soft milled flour, rye flours, grains of corn, rice and malted wheat kernels are selected from traditional mills in England, France and Ireland for Baker & Spice breads. In all, more than a dozen different types of flour, much of it organic and stoneground, are mixed together in different proportions to create individual bread recipes. The blending of flours is a key to creating the 'wild-yeast' levains and poolishes (page 61) that raise doughs naturally, and which contribute significantly to the complex, slightly sour flavour of the finished breads. This is the application of learned practice, essentially artisanal skills which impose consistency on the loaves. There are no chemicals or genetically modified soya improvers to speed things up or make life easier, just the passionate application of knowledge and sheer hard work.

New breads are developed by imagining the finished loaf and then carefully constructing the mix of flours, liquids, leavening materials and techniques. Each bread is created with its own mix of sour starters or fresh active yeast, flours, grains and, in some recipes, fruit and fruit juices, vegetables, nuts, fresh herbs and oils. The sourdoughs are based on four different wild yeast cultures, selected for their proven ability to create healthy, vigorous starters. These vary in moisture content and flour type, and are cared for by regular refreshment and vigorous aeration, at programmed intervals in the bakery throughout each 24-hour period. The bakery works 18 hours a day, seven days a week, from 10pm until 7am the next morning, and then from 10am until 6 or 7pm. As many of the processes involved in making the breads take days, each baker will have a hand in the production of most of the loaves that are produced.

Unusually for a professional baker in Britain, many of the breads are made in small batches, so the techniques used and the amount of what is being produced are on a scale closer to domestic cooking than is typical. The skills of the bakers at Baker & Spice are encapsulated in this book. The detailed recipes communicate simply how to get the best results. Everything is explained, from the consequences of using different yeasts to the impact of working with different flours. You will learn how to replicate the steam-injection used in the bakery to achieve crusted loaves with a delightful chewy crumb. You will discover that working with wetter doughs delivers better bread, and that techniques for gentle kneading and turning improve aeration and texture. All the recipes have been tested in a domestic kitchen using non-professional electric and gas ovens.

Everything that is done in the bakery carries through usefully into the practice of the domestic baker, so this is the most practical of handbooks. It is not about the hard work of a professional baker, but a story of finding and giving pleasure through the making of delicious things for everyday enjoyment at home.

"Good bread is a beautiful thing — a joy to look at and a pleasure to eat. Good bread never cloys and we never grow bored with it. Bread is as honest and basic as it is emblematic and significant. As rice symbolises life in the East and no meal is considered complete without it, so bread is at the heart of Western civilisation. Give us this day our daily bread."

Essentials

The smell of freshly baked bread, its crackling-crisp crust, its texture when it is broken or sliced and the consistency of its interior crumb, make it an immensely satisfying and complex culinary assembly. Yet its constituent parts are no more than flour, water and yeast, tempered with a small amount of salt. As you bite into a piece of good baguette you experience all of these elements in a taste that combines an

underlying sweetness from the wheat, an almost imperceptible balancing sourness from the yeast and a stronger, contrasting slightly bitter note from the caramelised crust – the whole drawn together and given depth by the salt.

A sourdough brings different and much stronger flavours, its defining characteristic the acid tang that comes from its lengthy, natural leavening with wild yeasts, the texture altogether denser, more robust and substantial. This is the darker-coloured country bread of ancient tradition, moister, more chewy and longer lasting, a description that in contemporary usage implies chemical additives but here means the product of its entirely natural development. Such rustic loaves were originally baked in 4 kilo ovals, family bread to last a week, changing in taste and texture with progressive cutting and ageing, yet taking days before staling. Even when too tough to chew, it may be eaten in soups or crumbed to add texture or to thicken a variety of dishes. This is indeed bread as the staff of life.

Baking great bread does have a kind of alchemy, for in its artisanal production there are always elements that are beyond technique, though not beyond technical comprehension. Ambient factors play important roles but are not beyond the wit of any competent cook to understand and harness. Even when the same recipe is used, the resulting bread will vary from place to place as different flours, the water used, temperature, humidity and even air pressure impact in different ways. Individual technique also plays a part, all these things contributing to the unique quality of the finished loaf.

Excellent bread is not only baked by master bakers. It can be made successfully at home and in standard domestic ovens. The specialist's oven frequently incorporates controllable steam injection and it is this steam that helps to form a perfect crust while preventing that crust from being impossibly hard. Most of the breads that we tend to regard as the exclusive preserve of the professional, such as baguettes and sourdoughs, or loaves baked in direct contact with the stone floor of a cavernous bread oven, can, in fact, be produced in any oven capable of high heat and using a baking stone, steam being generated by spraying water from a bottle.

As with any area of cooking expertise, great bakers have a vocation, and part of it is the ability to communicate how to achieve good and consistent results and to help others find pleasure in the processes of bread's creation. This book is about how to bake good bread at home. With practice, it can become great bread that changes the quality of any and every meal for the better.

FLOUR

Without good flour there can be no good bread. Skill alone cannot achieve it. Flour may be defined as the finely ground meal of any edible grain, though a reasonable assumption today is that it will probably be made from wheat. A description of such generalisation, arguably, obscures more than it clarifies. What makes one flour good or appropriate for a given task may make it unsuitable for another. A bag of soft self-raising flour, with chemical improvers and raising agents, is unquestionably a white wheat flour, but it is not the stuff from which a good loaf can be made. It may, however, conversely and perversely, be used to bake a decent cake and perhaps a reasonable soda bread.

The history of baking is at least 6000 years old, though what was called bread at different periods during that time has varied hugely from the earliest coarse-textured flat cakes cooked on a griddle over an open fire to the airy complexity of today's perfect baguette baked in a steam-injected oven. Wheat is capable of being ground more finely than most other grains, a fact that has always been identified with privilege. The bread of the poor for thousands of years was grim coarse stuff of millet, oats, barley and rye, perceived by those with higher standards of living as a damning card of social identity. In hard times virtually anything might bulk the breads of poverty, including pulses, chestnuts, vetches, weeds and – when starvation loomed – sawdust and even clay.

As the superiority of wheat over other grains reflected social hierarchies, so its finest expression was seen to be an ever more refined flour with less and less husk and wheat germ left in. The whiter and finer the bread, the higher up the social ladder the eater was perceived to be. It is really only in the last 100 years or so that the beneficial role that those bits sifted out and discarded to achieve this cosmetic enhancement might play in diet and digestion has been recognised. This is evident in today's rapidly expanding market for breads that add value by deliberately including bran from the husk, nutty-tasting wheat germ and various other grains and seeds. From a

nutritional point of view, such 'wholemeal' loaves are not necessarily going to be much better for you unless, of course, your diet is deficient in B vitamins and fibre. Choice today between white or brown, chewy or finely textured, is really only a matter of taste.

A typical grain of wheat is approximately 5–6mm long and 3mm thick. It is made up of a multi-layered cellulose husk – the bran – which surrounds a hard centre, 20 per cent of which is the oily and vitamin-rich wheat germ. This is the embryo from which it germinates, the rest being the starchy endosperm that contains all the gluten-forming proteins the embryo consumes as it starts to grow. Millers begin by selecting and buying a number of different wheat varieties to create a mix that they can reproduce consistently. Infrared analysis determines key characteristics, including protein content and humidity levels. Cleaning involves brushing and the use of magnets to remove metal contamination prior to washing and drying before milling.

Since industrial roller technology was first developed in the 1830s by the Swiss, most flours have been steel-ground, a high-speed process that generates heat from friction and that damages various aspects of the flour, including the gluten level and the vitamins and enzymes found in the wheat germ. Roller milling passes cleaned wheat grains between a succession of ribbed steel rollers rotating at high speed in opposite directions, the bran and germ being separated and sifted out, leaving behind only the whiter flour derived from the endosperm. This is ground finer and finer with progressive sifting between each grinding – known technically as bolting – until an ivory-coloured and powdery flour results. The extraction of the oily wheat germ means the flour keeps better, but the flavour is less pronounced. Once milled and stored, flour bleaches naturally with time, but storing is expensive so this whitening is now usually achieved rapidly with chlorine gas, after which the flour may have tiny amounts of niacin, riboflavin, thiamin and iron added to compensate for the vitamins and minerals lost during steel grinding.

The ancient practice of grinding wheat between slowly turning stones, which has gone on uninterrupted for thousands of years – at first powered by hand, later by water mills and today by electricity – is once again becoming more common. As a more discerning market continues to develop, so higher quality stoneground flours, once only available to the baking trade or at retail through healthfood shops, are to be found in better supermarkets. Yet this remains a fledgling business when compared to France where some 2500 independent small mills operate – in Britain there are less than a hundred. The most significant difference between French and British flours is that the former are milled at a slower speed, resulting in flours that retain more of the wheat's gluten. British bakers tend to achieve higher gluten flours for breadmaking by adding harder imported Canadian flours to the bulk of home-grown flours, an expensive practice because of high import tariffs. The higher the protein level, the less bran the flour will contain.

White flours not described as strong are low in gluten, in other words 'soft'. As a general rule, flours for making bread are harder, the hardest containing as much as 14 per cent of the total weight as gluten-forming proteins. Some breadmaking flours, like the French T550 used for baguettes, are quite soft but have other important qualities, including a low water-absorbing quotient, that make them ideal for this application. Soft flours are mostly used with chemical raising agents in wet batters for making cakes or to make pastries. Flour described as self-raising is soft flour that includes baking powder and other 'improvers'. Improver is the trade name for any chemical added to a flour to accentuate a given characteristic, for example to slow staling or to encourage and accelerate a particular process, such as yeast activation. These are the standard tools of industrial baking, but they have no valid role to play in the artisanal or home baker's breadmaking.

So-called wholewheat or wholemeal flours are darker in colour because they are made using the whole grain or the endosperm plus some of the wheat germ and husk. The precise percentages determine how dark and strong tasting the flour will be. Wholemeal flours consequently have a nuttier taste, which is imparted by the oily wheat germ. The inclusion of wheat germ and bran affects more than taste and texture, impacting on the gluten action and resulting in a lower rise and a denser loaf.

In this book, we use several different flours, some on their own and others in combination. With French flours, the T numeral is a designation describing the degree of sifting from whole grain, from the coarsest wholemeal to the finest white. The T stands for *taux des cendres*, the ash level left behind after a flour has been incinerated in a laboratory at 900°C. The greater the amount of ash, the higher the level of bran in the flour. Thus the T550 of baguette flour indicates that 55mg of ash is left after burning 100g of standard white flour.

TYPES OF FLOUR USED AT BAKER & SPICE

T450	A soft, fine French flour which we use for most of our cakes and biscuits. Substitute any ordinary plain flour.
T550	French white baguette flour; finely ground, soft but with low moisture absorbency. You can substitute a mixture of low-gluten plain flour and strong flour – see individual recipes for specific quantities.
Italian '00' flour	Unlike the carefully regulated French T designations, the description of '00' applied to Italian flour is not an absolute description of a protein level. As a general rule it describes a relatively hard flour, typically used for pasta-making and bread baking, but different millers will produce flours of varying degrees of hardness.
Doves Farm organic strong white flour	A classic stoneground white flour from Hungerford.
Churchill strong white flour	A stoneground white flour, similar to Doves Farm.
Odlum's Irish cream flour	A white self-raiser and the best flour we have come across for soda bread. We also use it when making scones and cakes.

Farine de meule (T850)	A French light wholemeal, pinkish in colour with no discernible flecks of bran.
Farine de meule (T1100)	100 per cent wholemeal, this French flour includes all of the husk and germ.
Granary flour	100 per cent wholemeal with whole malted wheat and barley grains.
English organic wholemeal flour	100 per cent of the grain; a strong brown flour.
Campaillou	Developed in France in 1970, this flour includes malt and dried levain to give a slightly sour flavour; it also includes the yeast catalyst amyl amylase.
Farine de seigle	A French 100 per cent rye flour, dark and with a strong and distinctive taste; its inclusion in a loaf changes the colour appreciably while the chemical make-up of the rye grain inhibits gluten action in the wheat flour with which it is mixed, producing a denser texture.

BASIC ELEMENTS

What kind of yeast? For recipes that are raised with active yeast, we always use fresh yeast in the bakery, but in adapting recipes for this book we have opted for fast-action, or easy-blend, yeast instead. Fast-action yeast is universally available, completely reliable and absolutely consistent. If you wish to use fresh yeast, simply double the quantity. So, a 7g sachet of fast-action yeast is the equivalent of 15g fresh yeast.

How much yeast? The amount of yeast used changes the rate at which fermentation and consequent rise take place and the texture

and keeping quality of a loaf. The less yeast used, the longer a loaf will take to prove. Over-yeasting will speed up proving, but it will also produce a thin crust and bread that stales rapidly.

How warm should the water be? The temperature at which you add water to a dough must be determined by the relative temperatures of the other elements involved. Thus, if you keep your flour in a cold place and the bowl of the mixer is cold, you need to compensate by making the water hotter and by warming the mixing bowl. Aim for a dough temperature of 22–24°C. Whether your kitchen is cold or hot will also make a difference.

Is room temperature critical? Ambient temperature is a key determining feature in yeast activity. While yeasts work at temperatures as low as 3°C, the majority of doughs are raised at temperatures that maximise fermentation. When a very warm environment is called for, the airing cupboard with a typical temperature of 28–30°C is ideal. All other times, a 'warm place' means a temperature around 20–23°C, draught-free. Where specific temperatures are required, this is always spelled out in the recipes.

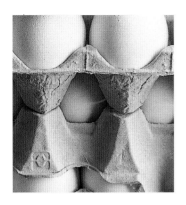

What size eggs should you use? Our recipes use medium eggs, which can weigh anything from 53g to 63g. We've assumed an average weight of 60g.

What's the best type of salt to use? We use Maldon, the best flake sea salt in the world. To assist its even distribution throughout the dough, it is worth blitzing a boxful in a food processor to give a uniform grind. Of course, this fine salt has many other uses.

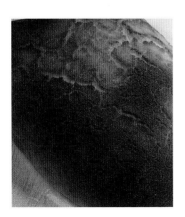

Does the type of water matter? We prefer to use bottled still spring water. This does not rule out the use of tap water, but bottled water is less likely to contain chlorine or other chemicals that might well impede yeast activity. This is particularly important with wild yeasts which are sensitive to chemicals, even in very low concentrations. Organic ingredients are recommended for the same reason. The less contaminated a water and flour starter environment, the faster and more aggressively the airborne yeasts will culture and work.

How can you tell when a loaf is cooked? With experience, you can tell by smell, feel and appearance when a loaf is properly cooked. Any loaf will have lost a lot of moisture when it is sufficiently cooked and it is easy to check this. Weigh the loaf before it goes in the oven, and again when you think it is done – straight from the oven. The loaf should be ready if it is 20 per cent lighter than when it went in.

OVENS AND EQUIPMENT

The recipes in this book have been tested in standard, contemporary gas and electric ovens without convection. Before starting, invest in an oven thermometer and check your oven's maximum temperature. You may be in for a surprise. Even brand new and expensive ovens carry no guarantees that they will achieve the 250°C you really need for at least the initial baking of many breads. If your oven is more than a few degrees below this, get it checked by an engineer. Usually the cause is a faulty thermostat or that the oven has been wrongly calibrated. If the oven is new, you should have no difficulty in having this rectified. Even if it is out of guarantee, there are companies that repair and maintain ovens. A more difficult problem to overcome with an underperforming gas cooker is gas pressure. Your gas supplier should be contacted if this turns out to be the cause of an oven not achieving high temperatures.

As all keen cooks know, you never seem to have too much cooking equipment and there is always a use for another bowl, whisk or sieve. For baking you must have accurate scales. A powerful table-top electric mixer is another great asset. Strong flours demand strong and lengthy kneading, which is hard work done by hand.

Wherever possible, we have suggested the minimum rather than the maximum requirements. Thus, instead of the wooden peel used by bakers to slide bread into the oven, we suggest using a rimless metal baking sheet. A spray bottle or plant mister will provide you with a steam-generating capability, but be sure to give it a cycle in the dishwasher if it was previously filled with a cleaning product.

must haves

measuring jugs and spoons

scales (in 5g increments) – preferably digital

table-top electric mixer with dough hook, paddle or beater and whisk attachments

hand balloon whisks

food processor

selection of mixing bowls in different sizes

plastic containers for levains and poolishes (2 litre with lids)

wooden spoons, numerous

wooden board for shaping

metal dough scraper

plastic and rubber spatulas

palette knife

skewer

scissors

rolling pin

rimless metal baking sheet (for peel)

linen cloths and tea towels

oven thermometer

several heavy baking trays

non-stick Swiss roll tins

loaf tins, 500g and 1kg

silicone mat or non-stick baking parchment

scalpel or razor blade

pastry brush

water spray bottle or plant mister

wire cooling rack

optional, but helpful

calculator

digital timer

flour bench brush

flour dredger

pastry cutters

linen-lined baskets for proving

baking stone

large and small brioche moulds

crumpet rings

cake tin, 20cm round

piping bag and tubes

"Dough is not something that you just leave alone. It has to be nurtured. And yet there is alchemy in baking, acts of creation. You impose your will only up to a certain point because a dough can appear to have a life of its own.

I use the analogy of gardening to baking – you know where you want to get to, but the plants do things that are beyond your control. There is a natural balance in bread you should never lose sight of." DAN LEPARD

Handling bread doughs

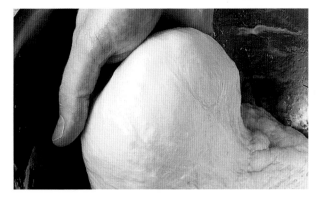

The way you handle any bread dough will determine how easily you control its shaping and development. It will also affect the rise and ultimately the baked texture. You should never be aggressive, which is why the standard British description 'knock back' is not used, since it implies a rather belligerent treatment. We encourage a more gentle approach, which pays dividends in improved elasticity by encouraging the formation of better distributed gluten strands and a better crumb in the loaf.

Making a soft dough

Many Baker & Spice breads are the product of very wet doughs, difficult to work with and untypical in British baking. They are too sticky to knead successfully by hand and can put an intolerable strain on the motors of table-top electric mixers. We have found, however, that by repeated but minimal kneading during an extended fermentation process you can aerate and develop the dough with little effort and to remarkable effect.

Essentially, we use repeated gentle deflations of the dough during the initial rise, something the French describe as *donner le tour* (to give a turn). To make life easier, we use some flour or olive oil so that you don't stick yourself to the dough. Each of the 'turns' lightly stretches the dough, as the yeast continues to work on the strands of gluten. By the last 'turn' we are left with a soft satin-like dough, free of any flour lumps and elastic to the touch.

MIXING THE DOUGH

Place the dry ingredients in a large bowl and add the yeast liquid first, then whatever other ingredients the recipe calls for. Stir with your hands until the mixture forms a rough ball in the centre of the bowl (1, 2, 3). At first, you will think the mixture is too wet and sticky, but don't worry – it is supposed to be. It is the high water content that helps give the bread its holes.

1	2
3	4

THEN, IF THE RECIPE CALLS FOR OIL

Tip a little oil on top of the dough and rub a little on your hands before starting to tuck the dough underneath itself (1). Rotate the bowl, not the dough, and each time you do, continue tucking the dough under with your fingertips until the mass feels smoother on top (2). Cover the bowl with cling film and leave it in a warm place for 45 minutes, or according to the recipe instructions. Repeat to make a satiny dough (3, 4).

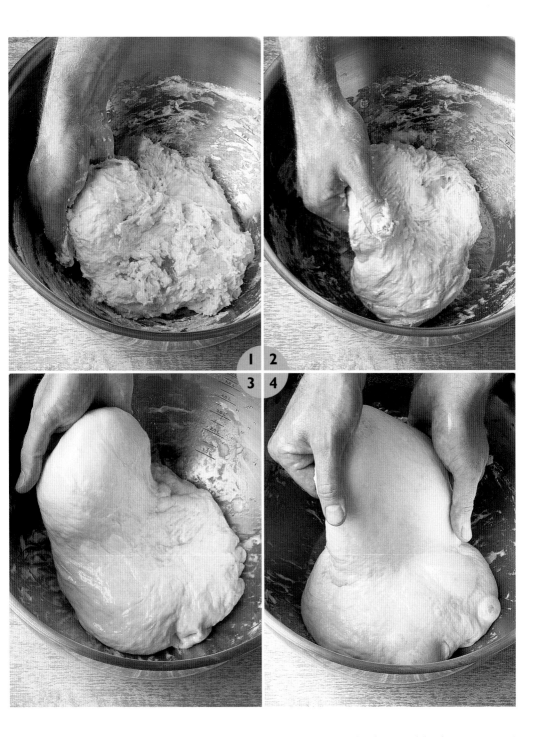

1 2
3 4

1 **2**

3

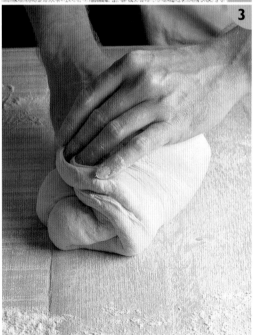

IF THE RECIPE DOESN'T USE OIL

Tip the dough on to a lightly floured surface and dust the top and your hands with more flour. Begin to tap the dough out firmly with the heel of your hand to form a rough rectangle, about 5cm thick. Fold in half (1), then in the other direction, in three (2, 3). Dust the bowl with flour and return the dough to it. Cover and leave in a warm place for 45 minutes, or according to the recipe instructions.

Whether you are using the oil or flour handling method, repeat the action as recommended in the recipe for the duration of the fermentation. By the end you will have a lively, soft and lump-free dough.

Kneading a firm dough

Kneading is not an art, but a skill that can be learned. When you watch a professional baker you will be astonished by the speed at which he works and impressed by the economy of his movements. A baker has to work fast because even in artisanal bakeries the output is staggering. Speed is not an affectation or showing off but a necessity, for without speed and focused energy the loaves would not be in the shop on time or in sufficient numbers for the customers to buy. Working in a domestic context the emphasis is not on speed – you are only going to be making a few loaves at a time – but on the kneading, and you will soon get the feeling for that. When you discover how delicious your own bread is and how little effort it takes to produce, this ceases to be a one-off exercise and you become a regular baker. Repetition and practice make for consistency in what you produce and the effort and time involved decrease. The only magic needed to create the same silky-smooth dough as a professional baker is a strong but light touch and an awareness of critical stage changes in the dough as you work it.

During the kneading, you change the structure of the dough with your hands, helping to create a uniform mixture, developing and distributing the gluten strands while stimulating the yeasts. Understanding the consequences of what you are doing and why you are doing it will help you develop the perfect method to get great results every time.

SOME BASIC RULES

1. Work quickly and on a wooden work surface if possible.

2. Keep your work surface very clean and dry, covered only by the lightest dusting of flour.

3. Keep your hands clean and free from sticky lumps of dough.

4. Dust flour on the work surface and your hands, and only on to the dough if necessary.

5. Be light but firm with dough, not heavy handed. Bread dough is tough and resilient and you must dominate it, not the other way round.

KNEADING A FIRM DOUGH

Lightly dust the work surface with flour and dust your hands, too. Tip the rough mass of dough on to the floured surface, then start to fold it into the centre (1). As you fold each corner in, press it down with the heel of your hand.

2

1

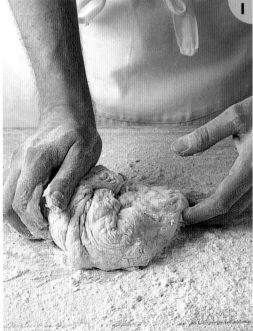

Rotate the dough a quarter turn, then repeat the process, until all of the rough edges have been folded in (2). Fold the dough over in half towards you, stopping it flipping back with your thumb. With the heel of your hand, press smoothly and gently into the mass, lifting your thumb away and turning the dough by a quarter in the same fluid movement. Do this again, concentrating on the process, the fluidity, the rhythm. Forget about the world for 10 minutes!

Just concentrate on folding, pressing down and across with the heel of your hand, turning the dough by a quarter, then repeating the action over and over (3). The texture will change and the dough become sticky. Then you'll need to scatter some more flour on to the surface and to dust your hands. How often you do this is not something you can write down. It comes from the feel of the dough in your fingertips.

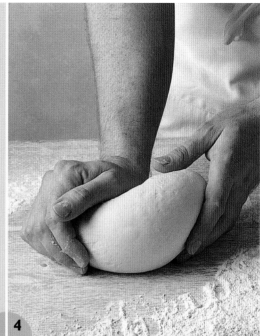

While kneading, break off from time to time to keep the work surface clean, using a scraper to remove any lumps of dough. Add a little flour as you need to – only to the surface under the dough and to your hands. Experience will tell you how often you need to do this. Eventually the dough will become beautifully smooth and elastic (4).

Shaping loaves

There is more to shaping than giving the raw dough a form which suggests that of the finished loaf. Different techniques are used for different shapes and the early kneading and folding contribute to the final form.

SHAPING A ROUND LOAF

Tip the dough on to a lightly floured surface and lightly flatten with your fingertips. Fold an edge of the dough into the centre and press it down firmly. Rotate the dough 20° anticlockwise and repeat the folding and pressing with another edge. Continue rotating and folding until all edges have been folded into the centre.

Flip the ball of dough over so the smooth side is facing up. Gripping your hands around the dough, drag and turn the ball firmly across the surface. Then pick it up, return to its starting place and repeat the action a few more times. This compacts the dough and helps the strands of gluten align – which in turn helps the bread to rise dramatically in the oven during baking.

SHAPING A BAGUETTE

Place the dough on a lightly floured work surface. (Too much flour on the work surface will hinder rather than help you.) Flour your hands. Tap the dough out with your hands to flatten it slightly. Fold the top edge of the dough to the centre and fold the bottom edge up to meet it. Press down with your fingertips (1).

2

1

Starting at one end, and in a continuous movement, roll the dough over towards you while closing the seam with the fingertips of your other hand as you work your way along its length (2).

Repeat this action two or three times until you have a seamless, sausage-shaped coherent mass. Finish by rolling with the palms of your hands, moving them from the centre of the loaf outwards (3).

As you roll with your palms outwards, apply an even pressure to encourage an even narrowing and lengthening of the shape (4).

SHAPING A BATON

Tip the dough on to a floured work surface and lightly knead into a ball. Tap out with your hands to form a rectangle. Fold the upper edge of the dough towards the centre. Press it down with your fingertips. Then fold the right and left ends of the dough in by 2cm, slightly on an angle so that the dough is vaguely triangular (1). Press these ends firmly to seal. Now fold the upper edge of the dough over to meet the lower edge and seal it down firmly with your fingers (2). Finally flip the dough around, so that the ends are reversed, and once more fold the upper edge over to meet the lower edge, sealing it down with the heel of your hand (3). Flip the shaped dough over so the seam is on top (4).

Shaping rolls

Rolls can be shaped from virtually any dough, though ours are typically based on pain blanc (page 96), delivering a nice, crisp crust with a light but chewy interior – perfect for splitting and filling or as breakfast or dinner rolls with butter.

SHAPING A ROUND ROLL

With practice, shaping a round roll should take just 5–10 seconds. First lightly flour the cloth you will rest the shaped rolls on. Weigh off a piece of dough 30–50g. Lightly flour the work surface and rub a little flour between the palms of your hands. If you are right handed, hold the dough in your left hand (1).

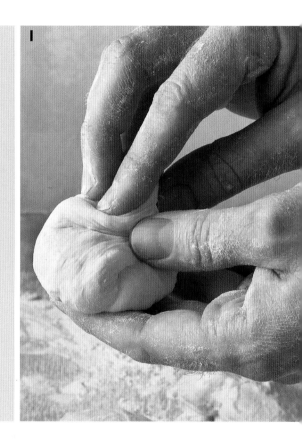

Cup your right hand around the dough, working the fingers under it. Circle this hand round and round, keeping your fingers underneath. Keep the palm that the dough sits in relatively free of flour and the hand that presses and rotates the dough well floured. Gradually the ball will tighten, and form a smooth skin on the upper surface (2). If you don't do this the roll won't hold its shape during baking. Place the shaped roll, smooth surface down, on the floured cloth. Shape the remaining pieces and place them face down on the cloth, leaving 3cm or so between each to allow for the dough to rise and spread.

SHAPING A LONG ROLL

First lightly flour the cloth you will rest the shaped rolls on. Weigh off a piece of dough 50–70g. Flour your hands and, on a floured surface, pat the piece of dough out into a rough rectangle. Fold the two upper corners of the dough in towards the centre, forming a triangular top with a flat base. Press these corners down firmly into the dough. Next fold the upper half down into the centre of the dough. With the tips of your fingers press the edge firmly down into the centre (1). Flip the dough around, so that the edge that was previously at the bottom is now at the top.

Again fold the top two corners in towards the centre and seal with your fingertips. Now fold the upper edge in towards the centre and seal it firmly down with your fingertips (2). Fold the dough in half and seal the edges with the palm of your hand, starting at one end and working along to the other. Turn the dough over so the seam is underneath. Cup your hands over the ends of the sausage shape, clawing your fingers around. Press down lightly and rock the dough gently back and forth, increasing the pressure on the edges of your palms so the ends of the roll are narrowed. Twist them into points.

Put the shaped dough, smooth surface down, on the floured cloth. Shape the rest of the pieces and place on the cloth, 3cm apart to allow for the dough to rise and spread.

"The first leavened breads were hit-or-miss affairs raised accidentally by the random action of airborne yeast spores. It was the Ancient Egyptians who discovered that the froth produced on top of beer during fermentation when mixed into dough caused it to rise, a breakthrough that meant bakers could control the process and achieve consistent results."

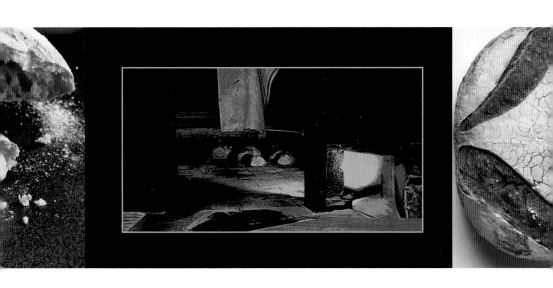

Baking with Wild Yeasts

Since the mid-1800s most breads have been baked using commercially produced cultured brewers' yeast which generates gas more aggressively than wild yeasts. It raises dough quickly and consequently produces sweeter, less tangy and lighter bread. Sourdough loaves, however, are still proved slowly using a starter dough colonised by wild yeasts.

SOURDOUGH BREADS

Sourdough breads are raised using the microscopic natural yeasts that are in the air all around us, and the breads get their name from the characteristic flavour they acquire during the lengthy fermentation and proving of the wheat flour dough. These are robust, rustic breads that keep well, and are often baked as very large loaves – the French oval-shaped *miche* typically weighs 2 kilos. Some cultures have always appreciated the unique taste, strong crust and chewy texture of sourdoughs. The French *pain au levain*, the Italian *pagnotta* and German rye breads are all examples of wild yeast baking at its best.

Bread has been raised using wild yeasts for at least 6000 years. How and why they made dough rise was not understood until 1857 when Louis Pasteur discovered that they generated carbon dioxide as a product of fermentation. When the type of wild yeast called brewers' sugar fungus, or brewers' yeast, settles in an appropriate environment, fermentation results, giving off carbon dioxide and delivering a distinct acid-sour flavour to the dough.

Brewers' yeast is the perfect leavening agent for strong, high-gluten bread flours because it generates gas slowly, over hours or even days. The gas is trapped as bubbles by the unique elastic and plastic qualities of the gluten, a combination of two proteins found in wheat grain. When moistened, they bind together to create thin, elastic strands. These form membranes that trap the gas, causing the dough to rise and producing leavened – as opposed to unleavened – bread. Putting raised dough in a hot oven makes the gas bubbles expand still further, and the dough cooks around them, leaving holes where the gas was and delivering light-textured loaves.

The first leavened breads were almost certainly raised accidentally by the random colonisation of airborne yeasts, until around 6000 years ago, when the Egyptians discovered that the froth produced on the top of beer during fermentation caused dough to rise when mixed into it. Other societies made the same discovery entirely independently, though much later. The Celts, for example, were found by the Romans to use beer froth, or barm, in breadmaking. In England, in the twelfth

century, dough was kneaded in a 'souring trough', which was never washed, so that the fermented dough left on its surface activated the next batch of dough. Beer froth continued to be widely used by bakers until the first half of the last century. Since then, most breads have been leavened using 'active', commercially produced yeast either in cultured or reconstituted dried forms. These raise dough quickly and consequently produce sweeter, less tangy and less chewy loaves.

Sourdough loaves, however, are still raised using a starter batter or dough colonised by airborne yeasts. The starter batters are called 'poolish' by bakers in the USA and Britain. This comes from the Polish of Poland, a country renowned more for its rye baking than its sourdoughs, but which exported knowledge and technique with its bakers as they moved first through Europe and then across the Atlantic. It is the lengthy fermentation of the batter that develops the acids, which give the bread its distinctive sour flavour. Levain is the term used for a naturally fermented old dough starter, the name levain being taken from the French *lever*, meaning to lift. The secret in baking these delicious and remarkable breads is in providing the right environment for the airborne yeasts to take.

The amount of sourdough poolish or levain a particular recipe needs has been adjusted to give optimum results. Many professional bakers use a strict 2 per cent of yeast to flour weight. At Baker & Spice we don't, because we feel such inflexibility only limits and restricts what can be produced. It is, however, always the start point when developing a recipe.

In the poolish recipes, precise ambient temperatures are given at different stages in the fermentation and proving process. This is not a science, however, and these are not absolutes, but the closer you can come to the recommended temperatures, the better the results will be. At all times keep the poolish away from draughts and try to avoid temperature fluctuation.

A poolish should not be cold when incorporated into a dough, so remove it from the fridge at least 2 hours before using. A levain, on the other hand, can be used straight from the fridge.

Wild
yeast starters

Making wild yeast starters is neither difficult nor
time-consuming, and has a satisfying quality about it.
All you need to do is create an environment that
airborne yeasts like. The magic is in the consequences
of the fermentation this produces. Some starters can
be kept going almost indefinitely – it is said that
sourdough starters have been handed down from one
generation to the next.

San Francisco sourdough starter

STAGE ONE

1 tbsp stoneground rye or wholemeal
   flour
300g strong white flour + extra for
   dusting
300g plain low-fat bio yoghurt
200ml apple juice
100g grapes or raisins, rinsed and
   drained

REFRESHMENT MIXTURE

150g plain low-fat bio yoghurt
150ml full-fat milk

BALANCE OF FLOUR

300g strong white flour

Put the flours, yoghurt and apple juice in the bowl of a heavy-duty electric mixer fitted with the whisk. On the slowest speed, beat for 10 minutes, when a slightly lumpy batter will have formed. Increase the speed and beat for a further 5 minutes, or until the mixture is thick, elastic and bubbly. Add the grapes or raisins, which will encourage the airborne yeasts to start working more quickly.

Pour and scrape the batter into a clean 3 litre mixing bowl. Dust the top with a handful of white flour and cover the bowl with cling film. Place in a very warm place (28°C) and leave for about 24 hours. This high temperature environment is necessary to kick-start the fermentation of the batter.

The next day the batter should have risen noticeably and may even have doubled in bulk. Beat for a minute with a hand whisk, then whisk in the refreshment mixture. When fully incorporated, pour the mixture through a colander into a clean bowl and discard the fruit. Now add the balance of the flour. Stir the mixture together with a wooden spoon for a minute or two, breaking up any lumps of flour.

Scrape down the sides of the bowl, then dust the top again with a handful of flour and cover the bowl with cling film. Leave in a warm place (about 21°C) for 24 hours. You now have an active starter that can be stored in the refrigerator in a plastic container with the lid on.

This starter can be used immediately, although it is better to wait, as it takes a couple of weeks for any special flavour characteristics to develop. Each day you need to refresh your starter – first remove 500–600g to bake with (or just discard this amount), then add the same mixture of yoghurt, milk and flour as before.

If you forget to refresh the starter, you will find that it separates and stops fermenting. It can be reactivated by beating in some more flour and yoghurt and a little apple juice. Alternatively, you can freeze the starter and reactivate it once thawed and at room temperature.

Our San Francisco sourdough starter, which is a poolish, uses yoghurt, as is typical in American artisanal baking. The poolish will raise dough as soon as the fermentation has begun, but we find that it takes a couple of weeks for a real flavour to develop. Bakers will give you pieces of wild yeast starter that have a developed flavour, and these can be beaten into the batter just before you add the fruit.

Vigorous and prolonged beating is important when making the starter, to incorporate the maximum amount of air. This will help to ensure that fermentation occurs quickly and aggressively. Later on, this activity is deliberately slowed as the emphasis shifts away from the generation of carbon dioxide needed to raise the loaf and towards the development of flavour and texture in the finished bread.

Biga acida

STAGE ONE
juice of 2 oranges
2 tsp wholemeal flour
60g Italian '00' flour
1 tbsp runny honey
100g strong white flour
100ml bottled spring water

REFRESHMENT MIXTURE
100ml bottled spring water
150g Italian '00' flour

Put all the stage one ingredients in the bowl of a heavy-duty electric mixer fitted with the whisk. Whisk at the slowest speed for 1 minute to mix, then increase to medium fast and whisk for 8–10 minutes.

Transfer to a large plastic container, cover and leave in a very warm place (28°C) for 24 hours. After this time the surface should be pocked with tiny holes as the yeasts start to activate. Leave for a further 24–48 hours to continue its development.

Pour the starter mixture into the bowl of the mixer fitted with the paddle and add the refreshment ingredients. Mix at a slow speed for 3–4 minutes, then return to the plastic container, putting the lid back on. Leave at room temperature for 4–6 hours, then refrigerate overnight. The poolish is now ready to use.

The Italian version of poolish, this starter is based on '00' flour which you can buy from Italian delicatessens and from some supermarkets.

Rye starter

STAGE ONE

125g strong white flour
125g stoneground rye flour + extra
    for sprinkling
150ml apple juice
150g plain low-fat bio yoghurt
50g currants, well rinsed and drained

REFRESHMENT MIXTURE

150ml apple juice
150g plain low-fat bio yoghurt
125g strong white flour
125g stoneground rye flour

In the bowl of a heavy-duty electric mixer fitted with the paddle, combine the flours, apple juice and yoghurt. Whisk at medium speed for 10–12 minutes. Stir in the currants and transfer the mixture to a plastic container. Sprinkle the surface with a handful of rye flour to make a 5mm deep layer. Cover with a lid but don't seal the container so it is airtight, then leave in a very warm place (28°C) for 24 hours.

The next day, beat the mixture in the container for 3–4 minutes, by hand or using a spatula or fork. Sprinkle a little more rye flour on top, replace the lid and leave for another 24 hours.

Sprinkle 1–2 tbsp rye flour on top, putting the lid back on as before. Once again, leave for 24 hours.

By the third day the mixture should be bubbly and have almost doubled in volume. Remove half of the mixture – this can be used in something like an American pancake batter or be just thrown away. Put the remaining mixture through a colander into a bowl, discarding the currants. It is now ready for the refreshment. Whisk together the apple juice and yoghurt, and add to the bowl together with the flours. Stir together, then return the mixture to the plastic container. Cover with the lid and put into the fridge.

Each day for the next 5 days, remove half of the poolish and discard it, whisk in the same refreshment of apple juice, yoghurt and flour, then return to the fridge to ferment. By the sixth day, the poolish is ready for inclusion in dough to be baked.

more information overleaf...

There is a strong tradition of dark rye breads in Poland, Germany and northern Italy. The greater the percentage of rye in a dough, the darker, heavier and stronger the flavour. This starter, which is a poolish, needs quite a lot of help to get it going, and it is essential to use organic ingredients – chemicals will prevent the yeast colonisation.

After a time in the fridge, the poolish may stop working. If it becomes sluggish and fails to double in size over 24 hours in the fridge, leave it in a warm place for 6–8 hours until it reactivates. It will gain strength from being refreshed every day.

Jason's basic French levain

STAGE ONE

100g strong white flour
40g wholemeal flour
3 tbsp bottled spring water
1 tbsp runny honey
40ml freshly squeezed orange juice

REFRESHMENT MIXTURE

4 tsp freshly squeezed orange juice
4 tsp bottled spring water
50g strong white flour
20g wholemeal flour

If you are making this starter by hand, mound the flours on a work surface. Make a depression in the mound and carefully pour in the water, honey and orange juice. Gently combine the ingredients with your fingers. As you work, the flour and water will turn into a paste, then into a ball of dough. Now knead the dough, but not too aggressively, for 7–8 minutes. When you have finished kneading, the dough will be resilient and will spring back when touched. If you are using a heavy-duty electric mixer (which will incorporate the maximum amount of air), put all the ingredients in the bowl and knead with the dough hook for 8 minutes at medium speed.

This dough is now a fledgling levain. Put it in a small, clean, dry bowl, cover with cling film and leave in a warm place for 2–3 days.

When the levain is ready, there will be evident aeration and a distinctly sweet smell of fermentation, and it will have increased in size by about half (opposite, left).

It is now ready for the first refreshment, which will give the yeast spores fresh material to work with. Dilute the orange juice with the spring water, then mix with the flours on the work surface to make a loose dough. Knead this together with the active levain until the two are thoroughly integrated. Put this in a clean dry container, cover with cling film and leave in a warm place for 15–20 hours. Your levain should now have risen appreciably and be full of bubbles when you draw a finger through it (opposite, right).

Repeat the refreshment procedure, using the same amounts, then cover the bowl with fresh cling film and leave at the same

wild yeast starters

temperature to ferment for 8–12 hours. By this time the levain will have doubled in size and have a slightly sour smell and flavour. It is now ready to use for baking. If you are not using it immediately, store in a covered bowl in the fridge.

This is an excellent starter, reliable and easy to maintain. Levain fermentation is much slower than that which occurs with active yeast, though using organic ingredients helps the yeasts to take and gets them working more quickly. Yeasts respond well to a splash of fresh orange juice, because the vitamin C acts as a catalyst. While this accelerating effect is initially desirable, the amount used in successive refreshments should be progressively reduced, as we do not want it to be too active in later stages.

Wild yeast breads

Breads made with wild yeast have stronger flavours than those raised using commercial yeast. With their more robust crust and chewy, well-aerated crumb, these are loaves with real character and individuality.

Pagnotta

MAKES 2 LOAVES

500g biga acida (page 66), at warm
    room temperature
250g strong white flour + extra for
    dusting
250g Italian '00' flour
125ml warm bottled spring
    water (about 20°C)

1 tbsp runny honey
1 tbsp Maldon salt, ground fine
olive oil for the bowl
polenta for the peel

In the bowl of a heavy-duty electric mixer fitted with the paddle, combine the biga and flours. Whisking at slow speed, slowly add the water and beat together. Change to the dough hook. Increase the speed to medium and beat for 8 minutes, when the biga will have broken down and the dough will be smooth and elastic. Add the honey and salt, and beat for another minute.

Rub the inside of a large mixing bowl with olive oil. Empty the dough into the bowl and turn it over several times to film the surface with oil. Cover the bowl with cling film and place in a warm part of the kitchen to prove. Leave undisturbed for 1 hour.

Transfer the dough to a lightly floured work surface. It may not have risen much by now, but the fermentation will accelerate over the next 3 hours. Dust the top of the dough and your hands with flour, then tap the dough out firmly with the palm and heel of your hand until it forms a rough rectangle. Fold in half, then in three in the other direction, until the dough is folded like a blanket. Return to the bowl, cover with cling film and leave in a warm place to prove for another hour.

Repeat the folding and deflating process each hour for the next 3 hours, re-covering the top each time with cling film.

Tip the dough out on to a floured work surface and lightly knead into a ball. Cut the dough in half. Shape each piece into a bâton (page 48). Flour two proving baskets and lay the loaves in them.

Cover the baskets with a damp cloth and leave to rise in a warm place for 3–4 hours.

Preheat the oven to 250°C, with a baking stone or heavy baking tray on the middle shelf. Test to see if the dough is ready for baking by pressing a finger lightly against the surface. The dough should slowly spring back to its original shape. Dust a rimless metal sheet with polenta: this will act as the peel.

Briefly spray the baking stone or tray and the sides and bottom of the oven with water, then quickly close the oven door. Upturn one basket so the loaf falls centrally on to the peel. Lift up the loaf and stretch it about 5cm lengthways. Set it back down on the peel. Hold the loaf on its peel next to the oven, open the door and swiftly slide the loaf on to one side of the hot stone, closing the door immediately. After 2 minutes, open the oven door and spray the bread and the sides of the oven with water, again quickly shutting the door to keep heat loss to a minimum. Repeat with the other loaf. Leave to bake for 10 minutes. Turn down the oven setting to 180°C and bake for a further 25 minutes, or until the loaves feel firm when pressed and sound hollow when tapped on the base.

Remove the bread from the oven and leave to cool to room temperature on a wire rack before slicing.

A classic well-flavoured loaf, this is baked with minor regional variations throughout Italy – the Italian version of a French pain de campagne. An experienced baker, used to working with wetter doughs could increase the amount of water to 150ml. The wetter the dough, the greater the aeration.

San Francisco sourdough

ILLUSTRATED ON PREVIOUS PAGES

MAKES 2 LARGE LOAVES

SPONGE
400g strong white flour
500ml warm bottled spring water
(about 20°C)
300g San Francisco sourdough starter
(page 64), at warm room
temperature

DOUGH
400g strong white flour + extra for
dusting
1 tbsp Maldon salt, ground fine
semolina for the peel

Put the sponge ingredients in a bowl and mix together with a hand
whisk. Cover with a damp cloth and leave in a warm place for 4–5
hours, when the sponge should be bubbling and obviously working.

Pour the sponge into the bowl of a heavy-duty electric mixer and
add half the quantity of flour. Using the paddle attachment, mix
together on a low speed for 2 minutes, or until the mixture begins to
cohere. Increase the speed to medium and beat for 8 minutes. Add
the rest of the flour and the salt. Change to the dough hook and beat
the dough for 8 minutes on low speed. Increase the speed to medium
and beat for a further 2 minutes. You should have an elastic dough
that will form a membrane when stretched between the fingers.

Tip the dough out of the bowl on to a 45 x 30cm tray. Lightly
dust the top of the dough with flour, cover with a damp cloth and
leave in a warm place for 1 hour. During this first fermentation,
sugars are broken down and converted to carbon dioxide and
alcohol. The gas provides the lift, but it is the alcohol that bonds
with the gluten as organic acids, causing it to contract. This makes
the dough more plastic and elastic, both resilient and stretchy.

Dust the work surface lightly with flour, and tip the dough off
the tray on to it. Rub a little flour on to your hands, then pat the
dough out to flatten it into a rectangle and gently deflate it. Fold in
half, then in three in the opposite direction. Flip this parcel over,
put it back on the floured tray and cover with a damp cloth. Leave
to prove in a warm place for another hour.

Repeat the folding and deflating process twice more, on the hour, then tip the dough out on to the floured surface. Divide into two pieces and shape each into a bâton (page 48). Line two proving baskets with tea towels and dust generously with flour. Lay the loaves in the baskets with the smooth upper surface down. Dust with more flour, then cover with another tea towel. Leave to rise in a warm place for 3–4 hours, when they will have almost doubled in bulk.

Preheat the oven to 250°C with a baking stone or heavy baking tray on the middle shelf. The plan is to bake both loaves at the same time, so dust two rimless metal sheets with semolina: these will act as peels. Tip one loaf from its proving basket on to a peel. Repeat with the second loaf on to the other peel. Open the oven door and slide the first loaf on to the back of the baking stone. Close the door (to minimise heat loss) while you get the second loaf, sliding this on to the front of the stone. Spray everything liberally with water, then quickly shut the oven door and bake for 10 minutes. Lower the oven setting to 180°C and bake for a further 40 minutes. Don't worry if the crust becomes very dark – the colour of the loaves will lighten a little after they are removed from the oven. The long bake helps the bread to keep better, preserving the texture of the crust. When done the loaves will sound hollow if you tap them on the base.

Transfer to a wire rack and leave to cool to room temperature before slicing.

San Francisco has been celebrated for its sourdough breads ever since the Gold Rush, when prospectors took pieces of starter dough from the city with them to the mountains of northern California to bake with. The name, sourdough, describes a loaf made primarily from white flour and raised with wild yeasts, but embraces different techniques.

wild yeast breads

Pain au levain

ILLUSTRATED ON PREVIOUS PAGES (TOP LOAF)

MAKES 2 LOAVES

100g strong wholemeal flour
400g strong white flour + extra for
    dusting
25g wheat germ
250ml warm bottled spring water
    (about 20°C)

50ml freshly squeezed orange juice
500g Jason's basic French levain
    (page 70)
1 tbsp Maldon salt, ground fine
sunflower oil for the bowl
semolina for the peel

In the bowl of a heavy-duty electric mixer fitted with the paddle, combine the wholemeal and white flours, wheat germ, water and orange juice. Beat at a low speed for 6 minutes. Now add the levain and continue beating for 4 minutes. Add the salt, increase the speed to medium and beat for another 4–5 minutes. The dough should be very elastic and quite firm to the touch.

Lightly brush a 3 litre mixing bowl with sunflower oil, put the dough into it and cover the top with cling film. Leave in a warm place to prove for 1 hour.

Transfer the dough to a lightly floured surface and knead for 8–10 minutes until the mass feels soft and elastic. Clean the bowl and lightly brush with sunflower oil. Return the dough to the bowl, cover tightly with cling film and put in a warm place to prove for 2 hours.

Turn out the dough on to a lightly floured surface. With the heel of your hand, pin out the dough into a rectangle to gently deflate it. Fold in half, then in three in the opposite direction. Each time you fold, press down to remove air. Dust the bowl with flour and return the dough to it. Cover and leave in a warm place to prove for 1 hour.

Repeat the folding and deflating process, then leave to prove for a final hour.

Divide the dough into two pieces, each weighing just over 700g. Lay a clean tea towel on a small tray and liberally dredge with flour. Shape each piece of dough into a tight, round loaf (page 45) and place 'gathered' side up on the tea towel. Pull the tea towel up between the loaves to form little folds of cloth around them. These will steady and protect the loaves as they expand. Dust the exposed tops of the loaves with flour and cover with another tea towel. Set in a warm place to rise until doubled in size, which will take 5–6 hours.

Preheat the oven to 250°C, with a baking stone or heavy baking tray on the middle shelf.

When the oven is at the correct temperature, uncover the dough. Sprinkle a little semolina on a rimless metal sheet: this will act as your peel. Take one loaf and gently place it, gathered side down, on the peel. With a scalpel, cut 4 shallow slashes in a square shape around the loaf, about one-quarter of the way down from the top.

Open the oven door and quickly spray the hot baking stone and the sides and bottom of the oven with water, shutting the door immediately. Carry the loaf on its peel to the oven and slide it on to one end of the hot baking stone, immediately shutting the oven door. Repeat with the second loaf. After both loaves have been in the oven for 5 minutes, reduce the oven setting to 200°C and bake for a further 55–60 minutes. When the loaves have finished baking they will be dark brown, will feel firm when pressed, and sound hollow when tapped on the base.

Transfer to a wire rack to cool to room temperature before slicing.

A classic, thick-crusted pain au levain is a long-lasting rustic bread. It has a terrific depth of flavour and a moist yet firm and springy crumb, with a texture more compact than some country-style breads.

Bramley apple sourdough

ILLUSTRATED ON PAGES 80–1 (BOTTOM LOAF)

MAKES 2 LOAVES

250g rye starter (page 67), at warm
  room temperature

1/2 sachet fast-action yeast (optional)

200ml warm bottled spring water
  (about 20°C)

375g strong white flour + extra for
  dusting

125g strong wholemeal flour

50g rye flour

2 tbsp apple juice

2 tsp Maldon salt, ground fine

200g Bramley's apples (peeled
  weight)

sunflower oil for the bowl

semolina for the peel

Whisk the starter and yeast into the warm water with half of the
white flour. Cover and leave in a warm place for 1 hour, or until the
mixture bubbles.

Place the remaining white flour in a 4 litre bowl with the
wholemeal and rye flours. Add the starter mixture, the apple juice
and the salt. Stir with your hands until the mixture forms a rough
ball of dough in the centre of the bowl.

Turn the dough out on to a lightly floured surface and knead for
8–10 minutes, or until it feels soft and elastic. Clean the bowl, brush
lightly with sunflower oil and put the dough back in, tightly cover
with cling film and leave in a warm place for 1 hour.

Peel, quarter and core the apples, then cut each quarter into 3 or
4 slices. Turn out the dough on to a lightly floured surface. With the
heel of your hand, pin out the dough into a rectangle to gently
deflate it. Press the apple pieces into the dough, about 2cm apart.
Fold one long side in by a third, then take the opposite side and fold
that over the first. Repeat the folding action with the ends. Dust the
bowl with flour and return the dough to it. Cover the top with cling
film and leave to prove in a warm place for 1 hour. Repeat the
pinning and folding process and leave for another hour.

Turn the dough out on to the floured surface, divide in half and
shape each piece into a bâton (page 48). Lay a clean tea towel on a
tray and liberally dredge it with flour. Place the loaves seam side up

on top. Pull the tea towel up between the loaves to form little folds between them. These will support and separate the loaves as they expand. Dust the tops of the loaves with flour, cover with another tea towel and leave in a warm place to rise until doubled in size, which will take $2^1/_2$–3 hours.

Put a baking stone or large baking tray on the middle shelf of the oven and preheat it to 250°C. When the oven is at the correct temperature, sprinkle a little semolina on a rimless metal sheet: this will act as your peel. Gently tip one loaf top side down on to the peel. With a scalpel, cut 3 shallow slashes at an angle at regular intervals along the top.

Working quickly, spray water on the baking stone or tray and on the sides and bottom of the oven, then shut the door. Fetch the first loaf and slide it on to the baking stone. Repeat with the second loaf. After both loaves have been in the oven for 5 minutes, spray them with water and lower the oven setting to 200°C. Bake for a further 45–55 minutes. The loaves have finished baking when they have taken on a strong colour, feel firm when pressed and sound hollow when tapped on the base.

Transfer to a wire rack to cool to room temperature before slicing.

Even the small amount of rye flour used here gives the bread character, without making it too heavy. The crumb is the perfect foil for the fruit, its sweetness balancing the acidity of the sourdough and making this a great bread to eat with cheese. This is a heavy dough, so you need an active poolish at least 4 weeks old. Extra lift can be given by the inclusion of some fast-action yeast. When Bramley's are out of season, use Granny Smith apples instead.

Potato and rosemary bread

MAKES 1 LOAF

250g biga acida (page 66), at warm
  room temperature
100ml bottled spring water
250g strong white flour + extra for
  dusting
100g baked potato flesh, cut into pieces

2 tbsp extra virgin olive oil + extra for
  oiling
1 tbsp chopped fresh rosemary
1 tbsp black onion seed (nigella)
1 tbsp Maldon salt, ground fine
semolina for the peel

Put all the ingredients except the salt in a heavy-duty electric mixer
fitted with the dough hook. Work at slow speed for 4 minutes, then
increase to medium fast and work for 5 minutes until the dough is
elastic and smooth. Add the salt and mix for a final 2 minutes.

Oil a 3 litre bowl, add the dough and rub the top with oiled
hands. Pull the sides of the dough down and tuck them underneath.
Repeat this 5 or 6 times, rotating the bowl as you do so. Cover the
bowl with cling film and leave to prove in a warm place for 1 hour.

Repeat the tucking process twice, proving for an hour each time.

Shape the dough into a round loaf (page 45) on a lightly floured
surface. Line a proving basket with a tea towel, dust liberally with
semolina and put the loaf in, smooth upper surface down. Dust the
loaf with more semolina, then cover with another tea towel. Set in a
warm place to rise until doubled in size, which will take 4 hours.

Put a baking stone or large heavy baking tray on the middle shelf
of the oven and preheat the oven to 250°C. Scatter semolina on a
rimless metal sheet: this will act as a peel. Using the tea towel, roll
the loaf on to your hand, then lay it, top side down, on the peel.

Spray the hot stone or tray, sides and base of the oven with water
then quickly shut the door. Leave for a minute to create steam, then
slide the dough off the peel on to the stone and shut the door.
After 5 minutes reduce the setting to 200°C. Bake for a further
45–55 minutes until the bread is a good colour with a firm crust and
it sounds hollow when tapped on the base. Transfer to a wire rack,
brush the top lightly with olive oil and cool to room temperature.

This is adapted from a recipe given to Gail Stephens by Erez Komarovsky, whose bakery in Tel Aviv produces extraordinary sourdough breads. The loaf retains all the freshness and big flavours of the original, but it is identifiably Baker & Spice.

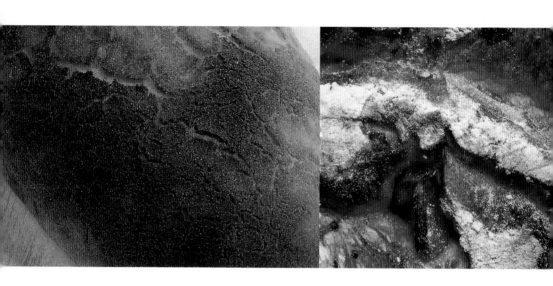

"Good bread is more than an accompaniment or adjunct to other foods, for it helps to shape our enjoyment and perception of the dish we are eating it with. Soup, charcuterie and cheese are all reduced in its absence. A sandwich, no matter how fine the filling, can only ever be as good as the slices of bread that define it."

Baking with commercial yeast

Cultured bakers' yeast (or brewers' yeast) is commonly used in commercial leavening. This fresh yeast is made up of the living cells of the yeast strain *Saccharomyces cerevisiae* and is usually sold as moist, compressed cakes which will keep for several weeks in a fridge. Although it is getting easier to buy fresh yeast, more predictable results are achieved at home using dried yeast.

USING DRIED YEAST

1. We have used dried yeast rather than fresh yeast in these recipes because it gives more consistent results in a domestic kitchen.

2. Dried yeast comes in the form of granules and is sold in tubs or packs of sachets. Available from supermarkets, it is variously described as fast-action, easy-blend or fermipan.

3. Dried yeast can be mixed in with all the other dry ingredients, but we prefer to make a sponge of the yeast, a little flour and some liquid. This speeds the initial fermentation and results in a better loaf.

baking with commercial yeast

Organic wholemeal bread

ILLUSTRATED ON PREVIOUS PAGES

MAKES 2 LARGE LOAVES

I sachet fast-action yeast
600ml warm bottled spring water
 (about 20°C)
550g strong white flour + extra for
 dusting
500g strong wholemeal flour

20g bran flakes
20g Maldon salt, ground fine
100ml freshly squeezed orange juice
rolled oats for coating
sunflower oil for the bowl and tins

In a large bowl, whisk together the yeast and warm water until the yeast has dissolved, then stir in 300g of the white flour. Leave in a warm place for 20–30 minutes, or until the mixture froths.

Put all of the dry ingredients, including the remaining white flour, into a 4 litre bowl. Add the frothy yeast batter and the fresh orange juice. Stir with your hands, mixing to form a rough ball of dough. Transfer it to a lightly floured work surface and knead for 8–10 minutes, or until the mass feels soft and elastic. It is hard work, but good exercise.

Clean the bowl and lightly brush with oil. Put the dough in the bowl, tightly cover the top with cling film and leave to prove in a warm place for 1–1¹/₂ hours. The dough should have risen, although it won't quite double in bulk. If you cut into a corner of the dough, you should see bubbles forming inside.

Lightly oil two 1kg loaf tins. Wet a tea towel and lay it out on the work surface. Lay another tea towel next to this and sprinkle it with a layer of oats.

Turn the dough on to a lightly floured surface. Divide the dough into two pieces and shape each into a bâton (page 48). Gently roll each shaped loaf on the dampened towel to moisten it, then roll in the oats to coat all over. Drop a loaf into each prepared tin, then cover with a clean tea towel. Leave in a warm place to rise until doubled in size, which will take 1–1^1/$_2$ hours.

Preheat the oven to its maximum – at least 250°C, the hotter the better.

Check the dough by poking it with a finger and watching how slowly the mark disappears. You are looking for it to come back slowly to its previous shape, but it must have some spring left in it, not an exhausted, last-gasp return. The loaves will continue to expand for the first 10–15 minutes in the oven, and will need reserves of undeveloped gluten to do this.

Spray the inside of the oven generously with water, then quickly shut the door. Carry the loaves to the oven and slide them in quickly, immediately shutting the door. After 5 minutes, reduce the oven setting to 200°C and bake for a further 45–55 minutes, or until the loaves are well coloured, have a firm crust and sound hollow when you tip them out of the tin and tap the base. Transfer to a wire rack to cool to room temperature before slicing.

This dense-textured bread slices well for sandwiches or toast. It can be baked in a tin to give a traditional English loaf or shaped as a free-form oval if you prefer. All the ingredients in the Baker & Spice loaf are organic, though you can, of course, use non-organic materials.

Pain blanc

ILLUSTRATED ON PAGE 99

MAKES 4 BAGUETTES

SPONGE

1/2 sachet fast-action yeast
175ml warm bottled spring water
  (about 20°C)
75g plain white flour
100g strong white flour

DOUGH

175ml cold bottled spring water
  (about 10°C)
1/2 sachet fast-action yeast
250g strong white flour + extra for
  dusting
125g plain white flour
10g Maldon salt, ground fine
sunflower oil for the bowl
semolina for the peel

Make the sponge: in a 2 litre bowl, whisk together the yeast and warm water until the yeast has dissolved. Stir in the flours. Cover the bowl with cling film and leave in a warm place for 2 hours, or until the sponge has risen by at least one-third and is clearly active, with lots of bubbles.

To make the dough, pour the sponge into the bowl of a heavy-duty electric mixer fitted with the whisk. Add the cold water and yeast and whisk at slow speed for a minute, or until the sponge is fully combined with the water. Change the whisk for the dough hook. Add the flours for the dough and work at a low speed until a rough ball of dough forms around the hook, about 2–3 minutes. Then add the salt, turn the machine up to medium fast and knead for 9–10 minutes, or until the dough is smooth and quite elastic. Transfer the dough to a lightly oiled bowl and cover the top with cling film. Leave in a warm place for 30–40 minutes, just time for the dough to relax.

Tip the dough on to a floured surface, ideally a large wooden board. Divide the dough into four, each piece weighing roughly 170g. Shape each lightly into an oval and place smooth side down on a floured dinner plate. Cover with a damp cloth and set aside in a cool place to rest for 15 minutes.

continued overleaf...

baking with commercial yeast

The special texture of a baguette comes from slow-milled French flour T550, also known simply as 'baguette flour'. However, we've found that a combination of low-gluten plain flour and strong flour will deliver a very acceptable – if not authentic – baguette in a domestic oven.

Baguettes are made using a two-stage leavening: the sponge is made with half the active yeast, with the rest added later during kneading. The trick when using soft flours for yeast dough is to keep the dough temperature quite cold. This is best achieved by mixing with cold water.

Other factors critical to achieving the brittle crust and light, open texture of a good baguette are the temperature of the initial dough and the maximum heat your oven can achieve at the start of baking. Steam – created with a spray bottle – is also important.

Achieving the right shape does not require the use of metal moulds – their use in large-scale commercial production is frowned upon by every artisanal baker. By simply rucking a cloth between pieces of dough you can achieve an authentic shape.

Take a large tea towel or linen cloth and sprinkle flour on the surface. Lightly shake off any excess flour, then lay the cloth, flour side up, on a large tray. Pull up the cloth every 5cm to create folds about 5cm high.

Take one piece of dough and place it smooth side down on the lightly floured work surface. Shape it into a baguette (page 46). Carefully lift the loaf on to the floured cloth, setting it seam upwards in the depression of one of the folds. Repeat the shaping with the remaining pieces of dough. (Alternatively, shape into rolls, page 51.) When they are all on the floured cloth, cover them with a slightly damp cloth to protect them from the dry air. Leave to rise in a cool, draught-free place for about 2 hours, or until doubled in bulk.

Put a large baking stone or heavy baking tray on a centrally positioned rack in the oven, and preheat the oven to maximum – at least 250°C or, if possible, 280°C.

Scatter some semolina on a rimless metal tray, which will act as your peel. Using the cloth to help you, roll the first loaf top side down on to the peel or tray. With a scalpel, cut 5–7 shallow slashes at an angle at regular intervals along the top.

Open the oven door and spray the baking stone or tray and interior of the oven with water, then quickly close the door. Carry the first loaf to the oven and slide it on to the far side of the baking stone, closing the door quickly again. Repeat with the other loaves, shutting the door in between each loading. When the baguettes have been in the oven for 3–4 minutes, spray them with water.

After they have baked for 10 minutes, lower the oven setting to 200°C. Bake for a further 15–20 minutes, or until the baguettes have taken on a strong, golden colour, the crust feels firm and the loaves sound hollow when you tap them on the base. (Rolls will take 30–35 minutes total baking time.) Transfer to a wire rack to cool.

French wheaten rye

ILLUSTRATED ON PAGE 102

MAKES 2 LOAVES

1/2 sachet fast-action yeast

150ml warm bottled spring water (about 20°C)

200g strong white flour + extra for dusting

50g rye flour + extra for the cloth

1 1/2 tsp Maldon salt, ground fine

280g rye starter (page 67), at warm room temperature

sunflower oil for the bowl

semolina for the peel

First make the sponge. In a large bowl, whisk together the yeast and warm water until the yeast has dissolved. Stir in 150g of the white flour. Cover the bowl with cling film and leave in a warm place for 2 hours, or until the sponge has risen by at least one-third and is clearly active, with lots of bubbles.

Put the rest of the white flour, the rye flour, salt and rye starter into the bowl of a heavy-duty electric mixer fitted with the dough hook. Add the sponge and turn on the mixer, to medium-fast speed. Mix for about 5 minutes, when the dough will have formed a rough ball. Increase the speed to maximum and mix for a further 2 minutes. Transfer the resulting sticky dough to a lightly oiled bowl. Cover the top with cling film and put in a warm place to prove for 2 hours.

Take a large linen cloth or tea towel, about 50 x 40cm, and lay it on a tray. Rub some rye flour into it and reserve.

Tip the dough out on to a lightly floured work surface and tap it out with your hands to form a rough rectangle about 24 x 18cm. Shape into a bâton (page 48).

Put the dough, seam side down, on the floured cloth. Cover with another cloth and leave in a warm place to rise for 3 1/2–4 hours.

Preheat the oven to maximum – at least 250°C – with a baking stone or heavy metal baking tray on a centrally positioned rack. Sprinkle semolina on a rimless metal sheet to use as a peel.

Roll the loaf on to your hand, using the cloth to help, so the base is on your palm, then upend it on to one side of the peel. Working quickly, open the oven door and slide the loaf on to the stone, then immediately shut the door while you get the spray bottle. Spray the sides and bottom of the oven liberally with water, taking no more than 5 seconds over it to keep heat loss to a minimum. Shut the door immediately and bake for 10 minutes. Then lower the oven setting to 180°C and continue baking for 40–45 minutes or until the bread is dark brown and sounds hollow when you tap the base.

Transfer the baked loaf to a wire rack and leave to cool to room temperature before slicing.

This bread uses both dried yeast and a small amount of active yeast to get maximum lift into the intrinsically heavy dough. It has a distinctive rye taste, which is given further flavour and acidity by the wild yeast starter. In France, this is the kind of rustic, chewy, mellow bread that would be called pain de campagne.

Make 'fresh' breadcrumbs from slices of day-old bread to use for cooking. Remove the crust, then leave the bread to dry, uncovered, at room temperature for about 24 hours. The following day, blitz in a food processor. The resulting crumbs are ready to use, but still have a high moisture content (they would turn mouldy if kept in a jar). To dry them for storage, spread out on a tray and place in a low oven for 1–2 hours, then cool. They will keep in an airtight container for several weeks.

Alternatively, put slices of bread (crusts on) on a baking tray and bake at 150°C until browned, then blitz to a crumb. This produces raspings – the finest crumbs – best for coating fish cakes or any food that is to be egged and crumbed for deep-frying.

English granary and sunflower seed bread

ILLUSTRATED ON PAGE 103

MAKES 1 LOAF

$^1/_2$ sachet fast-action yeast
300ml warm bottled spring water
  (about 20°C)
100g strong white flour + extra for
  dusting
300g Granary flour
50g rye flour + extra for the cloth

150g Jason's basic French levain
  (page 70)
$^1/_2$ tbsp Maldon salt, ground fine
75g toasted sunflower seeds
sunflower oil for the bowl
semolina for the peel

Make the sponge: in a large bowl, whisk together the yeast and
100ml of the warm water until the yeast has dissolved. Stir in the
white flour. Cover the bowl with cling film and leave in a warm
place for 2 hours or until the sponge has risen by at least one-third
and is clearly active, with lots of bubbles.

Put the flours in the bowl of a heavy-duty electric mixer fitted
with the dough hook, and add the rest of the water, the levain, salt
and sponge. Turn the mixer on at the lowest speed and work for
about 8 minutes, when a rough ball of dough will have formed.
Turn the speed up to medium and knead for 4 minutes. Remove the
dough from the bowl and put it into a lightly oiled bowl. Cover
the bowl with cling film and leave to prove in a warm place for
1–1$^1/_2$ hours.

While the dough is proving, take a large tea towel or linen cloth
and rub a little rye flour into the surface, then lay it, flour side up,
on a large tray.

Tip the dough out on to a lightly floured work surface and deflate it gently by tapping it out with your hands to form a rectangle. Shape into a bâton (page 48). Place the loaf, seam side up, on the floured cloth. Cover with another cloth and leave to rise at warm room temperature for $3^1/2$–4 hours.

Preheat the oven to maximum – at least 250°C – with a baking stone or heavy metal baking tray set on the middle shelf. Dust a rimless metal sheet lightly with semolina, to use as a peel.

Turn the loaf out, seam side down, on to your hand, and transfer it seam side down on to the side of the peel. Open the oven door and quickly slide the loaf on to the baking stone. Shut the door and get your spray bottle. Open the door again and quickly spray the sides and bottom of the oven, taking no longer than 5 seconds. Shut the oven door and leave the bread to bake for 10 minutes. Lower the oven setting to 220°C and bake the bread for a further 35–40 minutes, or until it is dark brown in colour (the malt in the Granary flour will accentuate this) and it sounds hollow when tapped on the base.

Transfer the loaf to a wire rack to cool to room temperature before slicing.

A loaf of pleasing textural contrasts and strong flavours, good to slice for sandwiches. The use of rye flour and malt makes for a darker colour and closer texture. Other seeds can be used instead of sunflower to ring the changes.

Semolina-crust pain de mie

MAKES 2 LOAVES

1 sachet fast-action yeast
250ml warm full-fat milk (about 20°C)
250g plain white flour
325g strong white flour + extra for
  dusting
10g Maldon salt, ground fine
1 1/2 tbsp caster sugar
100ml cold milk (about 10°C)
40g unsalted butter, softened

SEMOLINA TOPPING

300ml warm bottled spring
  water (about 20°C)
1 sachet fast-action yeast
300g semolina or ground rice
40ml sunflower oil
40g caster sugar

In a large bowl, whisk together the yeast and warm milk until the yeast has dissolved. Stir in the plain flour. Cover the bowl with cling film and leave in a warm place for 2 hours, or until the sponge has risen by at least one-third and is clearly active, with lots of bubbles.

Add the strong flour, salt, sugar and cold milk and start to mix. With your fingertips, rub in the butter and mix to a rough dough. Turn on to a floured surface and knead for 10 minutes, or until the dough is very soft and pliable, and the surface feels silky to the touch. Cover with cling film and leave on the work surface for 45 minutes to 1 hour.

Meanwhile, for the topping, pour the water into a bowl and whisk in the yeast until it dissolves. Add the other ingredients and mix to a smooth batter. Cover and leave to prove for 2–2 1/2 hours.

Divide the dough in two and shape each piece into a bâton (page 48). Place about 10cm apart on a large baking tray lined with non-stick baking parchment. Cover with cling film and leave in a warm place to rise for 1 1/2–2 hours, or until almost doubled in bulk.

Preheat the oven to 200°C. Uncover the loaves and lance each one at three points along the middle with a skewer, to release trapped gas. Apply the semolina topping evenly with your hands. Bake in the centre of the oven for 15 minutes, then lower the setting to 175°C. Bake for a further 25–30 minutes, or until the surface is cracked and the loaves sound hollow when tapped on the base. Cool on a wire rack, then remove excess topping from the bottom edge with scissors.

baking with commercial yeast

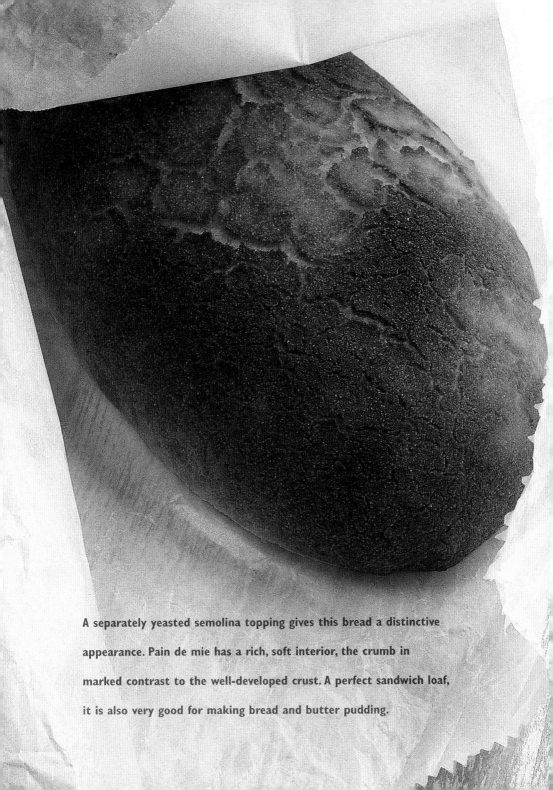

A separately yeasted semolina topping gives this bread a distinctive appearance. Pain de mie has a rich, soft interior, the crumb in marked contrast to the well-developed crust. A perfect sandwich loaf, it is also very good for making bread and butter pudding.

Dan's garlic bread

MAKES I LOAF

300ml warm bottled spring water
  (about 20°C)
425g strong white flour + extra for
  dusting
I sachet fast-action yeast
75ml freshly squeezed orange juice
100g Italian '00' flour
10g Maldon salt, ground fine
75ml extra virgin olive oil + extra for
  brushing
polenta for the baking tray

GARLIC FILLING

3 heads of garlic, separated into cloves
2 tbsp extra virgin olive oil
I–2 tbsp water
I tbsp balsamic vinegar
3 tbsp caster sugar
I tsp Maldon salt, ground fine
1/4 tsp black pepper
I sprig of fresh rosemary, leaves
  picked and chopped

Warm a 4 litre mixing bowl. Pour in the bottled water, then whisk in half of the strong white flour and all of the yeast. Leave in a warm place for 1½–2 hours, or until the mixture froths.

Add the orange juice, the remaining strong white flour, the '00' flour and salt, then stir with your hands until the mixture forms a rough ball in the centre of the bowl. The dough is supposed to be very wet and sticky: it is the high water content that helps to give the bread its open texture.

Pour one-third of the olive oil on top of the dough. Rub a little on the palms of your hands, then start to tuck the dough underneath itself. Rotate the bowl in quarter turns, turning the dough over and tucking under each time, until you have a smooth, shiny mass. Cover the bowl with cling film and leave in a warm place for 45 minutes.

Lightly deflate the dough with your fingers, making dozens of indentations. Zig-zag another third of the olive oil on the surface before repeating the tucking action. Re-cover the bowl with cling film and leave in a warm place for 30 minutes. Repeat the deflating and tucking process, adding the remaining oil and then covering as before. Deflate and tuck five more times (without oil) at 30-minute intervals – a total of 3 hours. By the end the dough should be soft and smooth with no discernible floury lumps.

To prepare the filling, blanch the garlic cloves in boiling water for 2 minutes, refresh briefly in cold water and peel. Put the olive oil in a small, heavy-based frying pan over a medium heat. When it shimmers, add the garlic and sauté for about a minute, being careful not to burn it. Add the water and balsamic vinegar and, as they bubble, stir in the sugar, salt, pepper and rosemary. Reduce the heat to its lowest setting and simmer for 5 minutes, when the garlic will be quite soft. Increase the heat and boil down the liquid until only a syrupy residue remains. Transfer the garlic to a bowl, scraping up all the syrup with it, and set aside.

Now you are ready to shape the bread, according to the illustrated step-by-step guide.

continued overleaf...

This is a remarkable bread, intense in flavour without being overpowering, sweet without being sugary, each bite a complete mouthful of contrasting textures and tastes. It is beautiful to look at, both as a whole loaf and as slices on a plate. Eat it on its own or to complement a simple, lightly dressed leaf salad.

Tip the dough out on to a floured surface and press out with the fingers and heels of your hands until you have a rectangle about 36 x 18cm and 2cm thick (1). Spread the cooked garlic and its syrup over the surface (2). Fold the long side furthest from you across by one-third (3).

Now take the opposite side and fold that over the first, trapping layers of filling between the folds (4). Repeat the folding action with the ends (5, 6). Flip the dough over, cover with a damp cloth and leave to rest for 30 minutes.

4

5 **6**

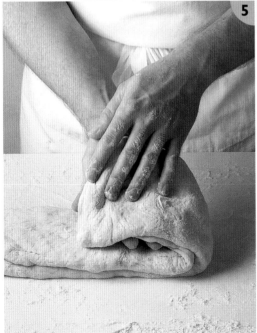

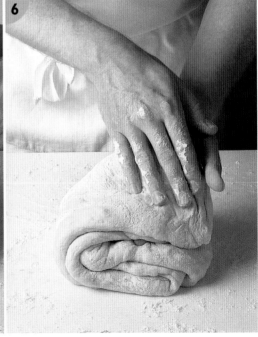

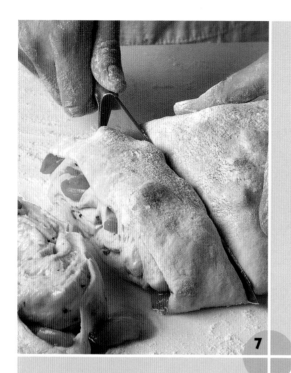

Brush a large baking tray with olive oil and dust with polenta. Using a sharp knife, cut the dough parcel across into 5cm slices (7) and lay them, cut side up, in a single layer on the tray, stretching each slice slightly into an oval. You can keep the slices separate, to bake individual small loaves, or arrange them so they are touching, in which case you will have a 'pull-apart' loaf, as with hot cross buns, when baked. Cover with a damp cloth and leave in a warm part of the kitchen to rise for 1 hour, or until almost doubled in size.

Preheat the oven to 250°C. Brush the top of the loaf with olive oil. Spray the bottom and sides of the oven with water, shutting the door while you get the bread. Place it, on its baking tray, on the middle shelf. After 5 minutes, lower the oven setting to 180°C and bake for a further 35–40 minutes or until the loaf is quite brown and blistered, and feels firm when pressed. Remove to a wire rack and leave to cool to room temperature before slicing and serving.

And if there is any left over the next day, slightly stale garlic bread makes a fabulous Mediterranean-style salad like panzanella: toast slices of bread on a ridged grill pan, tear into pieces and mix with quartered ripe plum tomatoes, chunks of red onion and fresh basil leaves. Slices of garlic bread are also delicious fried in olive oil and served topped with poached or fried egg and shredded fresh chilli.

Flat breads and shaped dough

Many flat breads, such as carta musica and tortillas, do not contain yeast. The flat breads here, while raised with active yeast, are distinguished from the majority of leavened breads in that the height or thickness of the bread is deliberately restricted, with the loaves having a much larger surface area in proportion to their depth.

Focaccia

ILLUSTRATED ON PREVIOUS PAGE

MAKES 2 FOCACCIA

1 sachet fast-action yeast
680ml warm bottled spring water
(20°C) + 1–2 tbsp more if required
1kg strong white flour + extra for
dusting
20g Maldon salt, ground fine
1 tsp caster sugar
1 tbsp olive oil + more for brushing

TO FINISH

leaves from 2 sprigs of fresh rosemary
(about 1 heaped tbsp), optional
75ml extra virgin olive oil
coarse Maldon sea salt

Make the sponge: in a large bowl, whisk together the yeast and warm water until the yeast has dissolved. Stir in 500g of the flour. Cover the bowl with cling film and leave in a warm place for 2 hours, or until the sponge has risen by at least one-third and is clearly active, with lots of bubbles.

Put the remaining flour in the bowl of a heavy-duty electric mixer fitted with the dough hook and add the sponge, salt, sugar and oil. Mixing at the lowest speed, work for 7 minutes. If the dough is too stiff, add a little more water, 1 tbsp at a time. It should be firm and slightly sticky. Increase to full speed and beat for 1 minute, when you should have an elastic dough that is resilient to the push of a finger and which springs back when you stop pushing.

Turn out on to a floured surface and shape into a ball. Oil a bowl large enough to allow the dough to treble in size. Put the dough in and brush the top with a little olive oil. Cover with cling film and leave to prove in a cool, draught-free place for about 2 hours. The dough will be moist, sticky and elastic as you take it from the bowl.

Transfer to a heavily floured work surface. Tap the dough out firmly with the palm and heel of your hand to a rough rectangle. Fold in half, then in three in the other direction, until the dough is folded like a blanket. Divide in half, and tap and press out each piece into a rectangle again. Transfer to 2 floured non-stick Swiss roll tins, each about 30 x 20cm, and push out to fill the tins evenly.

Cover each tin with a cloth and leave to rise at room temperature for 1 hour. Preheat the oven to 250°C.

With the tips of your fingers, poke holes in the dough to dimple the surfaces comprehensively in straight lines. Sprinkle on the rosemary, if using. Zig-zag the olive oil over and scatter coarse salt on top. Bake in the centre of the oven for 10 minutes, then turn the setting down to 200°C. Continue baking for 15–20 minutes, when the focaccia will have risen to a height of about 4–5cm. Remove and leave to cool in the tins. To serve, cut in squares.

Focaccia is described as an Italian flat bread, though it is leavened using active yeast. The dough is spread out and baked on trays or in tins, which gives it a rectangular shape, and the top is marked with regular depressions. It turns a beautiful golden brown from the liberal dressing with olive oil it receives just before baking. A common mistake is to incorporate too much olive oil into the dough itself, leading to a poor rise and an oily finish. Focaccia is always well salted on the surface and often includes rosemary.

Focaccia dough rolled out to thin rounds is perfect as a pizza base. Keep toppings to a minimum – the best pizzas have the most basic and simple toppings, like a classic margherita of tomato, mozzarella and basil. For baking pizzas, a very hot oven and a baking stone are ideal, though metal pizza trays also work well. Allow about 8 minutes in the oven.

flat breads and shaped doughs

Roast pepper and paprika bread

ALSO ILLUSTRATED ON PAGES 122–3 (BOTTOM LOAF)

MAKES I LARGE LOAF

3 large ripe red peppers
370ml warm bottled spring water
    (about 20°C)
1/2 sachet fast-action yeast
575g strong white flour + extra for
    dusting

10g Maldon salt, ground fine
50ml extra virgin olive oil
1 tsp paprika, dissolved in 50ml extra
    virgin olive oil
semolina for the baking tray

One at a time, thread the peppers on to a metal skewer and, holding the end in a cloth or oven glove, turn over a flame until the skin blisters all over and begins to char. (If you do not have gas, turn the peppers frequently under a preheated hot grill.) Put the peppers into a bowl and cover tightly with cling film. As soon as they are cool enough to handle, strip off the skin, working from the stalk end and using a small, sharp knife to lift and pull with. Cut the peppers in half lengthways and scrape out the seeds. Cut out the cores and white ribs. Set the peppers aside.

In the bowl of a heavy-duty electric mixer, whisk together the water, yeast and half the flour. Cover the bowl with cling film and leave in a warm place for $1^1/2$–2 hours, or until the mixture is frothy.

Place the remaining flour in a 4 litre bowl and add the yeast mixture, the salt and olive oil. Fit the dough hook to the mixer and knead the dough for 3 minutes on a slow speed, then increase the speed to medium fast and briskly beat the dough for 8–9 minutes, or until it is very smooth and elastic and has a satin feel. Cover the bowl with cling film and leave in a warm place to prove for 45 minutes.

Tip the dough out on to a floured work surface. Lightly sprinkle a little flour over the surface of the dough, and rub a little more on your hands. Tap the dough out firmly with the palm and heel of your hand until it forms a rough rectangle.

continued overleaf...

Fold the dough in half, then in three in the other direction, until it is folded like a blanket. Each time you fold, press down to remove air. Dust the bowl with flour and return the dough to it. Cover and leave to prove in a warm place for 30 minutes. Repeat the folding and deflating every 30 minutes for a total of 3 hours. By now the dough should be soft, aerated and smooth.

Tip the dough out on to the floured surface. Shape it into a rough ball, leaving it seam side down. Cover with a cloth and leave to rest for 15 minutes.

Flip the ball of dough over smooth side down on the lightly floured surface. Tap it out with the palms of your hands to flatten it slightly, then shape it into a bâton (page 48). Cover the dough and leave to rest on the work surface for 15 minutes.

Now roll out one long side of the loaf with a rolling pin, creating a rounded, flat end that extends away from the rest of the loaf and is large enough to fold back and wrap round the piece which will form the base. With your fingertips indent the surface of the base only. Take the pepper halves and lay them over the indentations, leaving a 2cm edge uncovered. Brush the peppers with a little of the paprika oil.

With a scalpel, slash through the rolled-out lid, creating a herringbone of cuts. Carefully lift this and wrap it over the top of the loaf, so that the peppers are slightly exposed through the lattice. Tuck around the dough so that the lattice is firmly in place. Line a heavy baking tray with non-stick baking parchment or a silicone mat and sprinkle with semolina. Transfer the loaf to the tray. Leave in a warm part of the kitchen to rise for 45 minutes to 1 hour, or until almost doubled in size. Preheat the oven to 250°C.

Brush the top of the loaf with the remaining paprika oil. Bake for 15 minutes, then reduce the oven setting to 180°C and bake for a further 30–35 minutes, or until the loaf is well browned and slightly blistered and feels firm when touched.

Remove from the tray and leave to cool on a wire rack.

Paprika, originally a Hungarian spice, is the fine powder made from a dried variety of sweet red pepper which, although it looks like a large chilli, has no real heat. A similar though different-tasting spice is made in Spain where it is called pimentón. Either paprika or pimentón can be used for this recipe. It is worth investing in a good brand as there are many poor quality red pepper powders passed off as the real thing – if it is cheap it is almost certainly not worth buying. Paprika and pimentón should be dark, brick-red in colour and have a strong, smoky smell. If the spice is brown rather than red, it is stale and should not be used.

Roquefort and walnut fougasse

ILLUSTRATED ON PREVIOUS PAGES (TOP LEFT)

MAKES 3 FOUGASSES

SPONGE
170ml warm bottled spring water
(about 20°C)
170g strong white flour
1/2 sachet fast-action yeast

DOUGH
270ml warm bottled spring water
(about 20°C)
1/2 sachet fast-action yeast
450g strong white flour + extra for
dusting

120g rye flour
10g Maldon salt, ground fine
1 tbsp extra virgin olive oil + extra for
brushing

ROQUEFORT AND WALNUT FILLING
200g Roquefort, crumbled
150g walnuts, toasted in a 180°C oven,
then roughly chopped

Make the sponge (the fermented starter): put the water into a large
bowl and mix in the flour and yeast. Keep mixing for 3–4 minutes,
or until a smooth batter has formed. Cover with cling film and let
the sponge sit in a warm place for $1^1/2$–2 hours, or until it looks
active and full of bubbles.

To make the dough, add the water and yeast to the sponge. Then
add the flours, salt and olive oil, and mix to a rough dough. Turn the
dough out on to a floured work surface and knead for 5–8 minutes to
form a soft, smooth dough. Transfer this to a clean, dry container,
cover with a damp cloth and leave in a warm place for 30 minutes.

Return the dough to the floured work surface and pin it out into
a rectangle to deflate it. Cover the surface with the Roquefort and
walnuts, then gently fold the edges of the dough into the middle so
that the filling is enclosed. Repeat the pinning and folding action
several times. By this time the filling should be evenly distributed

through the dough. (For a plain fougasse, omit the filling, but fold as described.) Transfer to a lightly oiled bowl, cover with cling film and leave to prove in a warm place for 45 minutes.

Divide the dough into three equal pieces and shape each into a ball. Leave to rest on the floured work surface, covered with a damp cloth, for 15 minutes. Then roll each piece of dough out into an oval about 25–30cm long and 10–12cm wide. Cut 8 or 9 deep slashes in each oval, cutting at an angle. Transfer the fougasses to baking trays lined with non-stick baking parchment or a silicone mat, cover with cling film and leave to rise at room temperature for at least 1 hour. Preheat the oven to 220°C.

Brush the fougasses generously with extra virgin olive oil. Bake for 15–20 minutes, or until well coloured, with a firm crust. The bread should sound hollow when tapped on the base. Cool on a wire rack.

Perhaps surprisingly, the fougasse of Provence is derived from an Italian flat bread made in northwest Italy. It is a pretty bread distinguished by its slashed holes, traditionally cut in a ladder or tree shape, though they may form a rough herringbone pattern. Originally a sweet bread eaten as a dessert, fougasses are now more often plain or savoury.

Pretzels

MAKES 1 BIG PRETZEL

200g Pagnotta dough (page 74) or
Focaccia dough (page 116), after
proving and ready to shape
strong white flour for dusting
sunflower oil and semolina for the peel

TO FINISH
1 egg, beaten with 1 tbsp water
(egg wash)
1–2 tsp zatar or sesame seeds

Roll the dough into a cylinder, about 50cm long, on a heavily floured surface. Turn this to make a loop, as if making the first move when tying a tie. You will have an oval with one piece of dough crossing over itself, like a lapel ribbon. Twist the loop in the middle to give two equal loops above the crossed-over tails of the dough. Bring the tails up and over the loops, pressing down.

Flour a cloth-lined tray. Transfer the pretzel to the tray. Cover with another cloth and leave to rise in a warm place for 30 minutes.

Preheat the oven to 220°C, with a baking stone or heavy metal baking tray on the middle rack. Lightly brush a rimless metal sheet with oil and dust with semolina: this will act as a peel.

During rising the pretzel will have contracted as well as expanded. Tug and stretch it gently to restore it shape. Transfer to the peel and brush with egg wash. Scatter the zatar or sesame seeds on top of the pretzel, then slide it on to the baking stone and bake for 40–45 minutes. Remove to a wire rack to cool.

Our pretzels are big, New York-style twists of pagnotta dough dusted with sesame seeds or zatar, baked golden crisp but with a nicely light-textured crumb. Zatar is a Middle Eastern spice mix given a characteristic sour edge by sumak. To make zatar, mix together equal amounts of powdered sumak and powdered dried marjoram and thyme.

Grissini

ILLUSTRATED ON PAGE 127 (CENTRE)

MAKES ABOUT 25 GRISSINI

1 recipe Pagnotta dough (page 74) or Focaccia dough (page 116), after proving and ready to shape

strong white flour for dusting

semolina for dusting

TO FINISH (OPTIONAL)

50ml extra virgin olive oil

chopped fresh thyme, rosemary or oregano

25g coarse Maldon salt

coarsely ground black pepper

Turn the dough on to a floured work surface and flatten out with your hands. Lightly flour the surface of the dough, then roll out with a rolling pin into a long rectangle, as thin as you can. The dough will reach a point when it resists your best efforts and shrinks back. At this stage, cover with a tea towel and leave it to rest for 15–20 minutes.

Uncover the dough, roll out and rest, covered, a second time. Roll out the dough again, to a rectangle about 8–10mm thick.

Line two baking trays with non-stick baking parchment or a silicone mat and sprinkle with semolina. With a sharp knife, roughly cut the dough rectangle into 1cm wide lengths. Make lengthways cuts in one end of each strip of dough, if you like. Transfer them as you cut to the baking trays, leaving space between them. When you have used up all the dough, cover the trays with cling film and leave to rise at warm room temperature for 45 minutes to 1 hour.

Preheat the oven to 200°C. If you like, you can lightly brush the tops of the grissini with a little olive oil, then sprinkle them with a few chopped herbs, sea salt or black pepper – whatever takes your fancy. (At Baker & Spice the grissini are kept plain, covered only with a light dusting of flour.)

Place the trays in the oven and bake for 20–30 minutes, or until the grissini are lightly coloured and crisp. Once removed from the oven, transfer to a wire rack to cool.

Grissini — crisp bread sticks — were first made in Turin in Italy and remain a speciality of that city's small street bakeries. They bear little resemblance to mass-produced grissini, which are machine-made, more or less identical, smooth and snap to a tongue-drying dust in the mouth. Turin's grissini are closer to loaves, and some are up to a metre long.

Sweet yeast breads

The tradition of baking sweet yeasted doughs enriched with eggs and butter is almost as old as leavened bread. The products can range from relatively simple spice breads, often with festive calendar associations, like hot cross buns and pain d'épices, to luxurious brioches.

Hot Cross Buns

ILLUSTRATED ON PREVIOUS PAGE

MAKES 24 BUNS

1 sachet fast-action yeast

200ml warm bottled spring water
(about 20°C)

870g strong white flour + extra for
dusting

230ml cold bottled spring water
(about 10°C)

25g skimmed milk powder

100g caster sugar

15g Maldon salt, ground fine

85g unsalted butter, softened

1 egg

3–4 tsp ground mixed spice, or
more to taste

100g raisins

70g dried apricots, chopped

80g candied citrus peel, chopped

PIPING PASTE

4 tbsp plain white flour

1 tbsp caster sugar

1 tbsp cold water

GLAZES

1 egg yolk

1 tbsp milk

100g sugar

50ml water

Make the sponge: in a large bowl, whisk together the yeast and the warm water until the yeast has dissolved. Stir in 200g of the flour. Cover the bowl with cling film and leave in a warm place for 2 hours, or until the sponge has risen by at least one-third and is clearly active, with lots of bubbles.

Put the remaining flour in the bowl of a heavy-duty electric mixer fitted with the dough hook and add the sponge, cold water, milk powder, sugar, salt, butter, egg and mixed spice. Switch on at the lowest speed and work for 8 minutes, when you will have a very soft dough. Add the fruit and candied peel, turn up the speed to medium and knead for 1 minute only.

Transfer the dough to a floured work surface and knead for about 1 minute, then form a ball. Put into a bowl, cover with cling film and leave to prove in a warm place for 45 minutes to 1 hour, or until doubled in bulk.

Turn out on to the lightly floured work surface and gently press out into a rectangle to deflate. Divide the dough into 24 equal pieces and form each piece into a neat ball.

Line baking trays with non-stick baking parchment and arrange the balls on the trays in lines, almost but not quite touching. Cover with a slightly damp cloth and leave in a warm place to rise for 45 minutes, or until the buns have doubled in size and joined together as they have expanded.

Halfway through the rise, preheat the oven to 250°C. Also, make the piping paste for the crosses by mixing the flour and sugar with the water. Put into a piping bag fitted with a small, plain nozzle. Beat the egg yolk and milk together for a glaze.

Using a skewer or a blunt knife, indent a cross on the top of each bun. Brush with the egg glaze, then pipe a cross in the indentation. Put the buns in the oven, turning the setting down to 180°C as soon as you shut the door. Bake for 30–40 minutes, or until the buns are golden and darkening around the outside edges. Like bread rolls, they will sound hollow when tapped on the base.

Transfer to a wire rack. Dissolve the sugar in the water and bring to the boil. Brush this glaze over the buns. Resist the temptation to pull them apart until they have cooled to room temperature.

Sweet, moist, spicy and studded with fruit, hot cross buns are that British rarity — a seasonally baked speciality. Of course, they are just as nice without the piped Easter cross at any time of the year.

Brioche

ILLUSTRATED ON PREVIOUS PAGES

**MAKES 2 LARGE BRIOCHES OR
16 INDIVIDUAL ONES**

1 sachet fast-action yeast
500g strong white flour + extra for
    dusting
50ml warm bottled spring water
    (about 20°C)
15g Maldon salt, ground fine
75g caster sugar

5 eggs
250g unsalted butter, softened
melted butter and flour for the tins

GLAZE

2 egg yolks
2 tbsp milk or water

Make the sponge: dissolve the yeast and 25g of the flour in the warm water. Cover and leave in a warm place for 30–40 minutes, or until bubbling and clearly active.

Place the remaining flour in the bowl of a heavy-duty electric mixer fitted with the paddle and add the sponge, salt, sugar and eggs. Mix at low speed until the dough comes together – about 7 minutes. Add the butter, increase the mixer speed to medium and continue to mix for about 15 minutes, when the butter will be fully incorporated and the dough will be shiny and elastic. Transfer the dough to a lidded plastic container or cling-wrapped bowl and refrigerate overnight.

Put the dough on a floured work surface. Divide it in half, or for individual brioches, into 16 pieces each weighing 60g. Shape each piece into a ball and leave to rest for 20 minutes.

For each large brioche: divide the ball of dough into two uneven pieces, one about one-third of the total amount. Shape the larger piece of dough into a ball, then make a hole in the centre of the top with your finger and push down until you break through the bottom. Stretch the hole with your fingers until you have a rather fat and tall ring doughnut. Now shape the smaller piece into a cylinder tapered at one end. Cut through the tapered end from its end to halfway up. You should have a shape that looks a little like a tooth, with the split tapered end forming its roots. Place this end into the hole in the doughnut, pulling the roots through and tucking them under the base.

This will ensure that the head of the brioche rises straight up, and doesn't lean to one side. Tuck the top edge of the doughnut back into the hole, to keep the two pieces together as the brioche rises.

Or to shape individual brioche: using the edge of your outstretched hand like a knife, make an indentation in the ball of dough to measure off about a third. Lightly grip the large end of the dough ball with your other hand, and rock the dough back and forth, separating a smaller ball joined by a thread to the larger ball. Then carefully turn the large ball upright and shove your fingers into the top to make an indentation. Put the smaller ball of dough into it, coiling the joining thread underneath into the hole.

Lightly brush two fluted brioche tins (or 16 individual tins) with melted butter and dust with a little flour. Place the moulded brioches firmly inside the tins. Leave to rise in a warm place for 3–4 hours, or until doubled in bulk.

Preheat the oven to 200°C. For the glaze, lightly beat the egg yolks with the milk or water. Brush the top of the brioches with glaze. Bake for 10–15 minutes, then lower the oven setting to 180°C. Bake for a further 35–40 minutes for large brioches, 15–20 minutes for individual ones, or until risen and a good golden brown. Transfer to a wire rack to cool. Serve warm.

Brioche is the most luxurious of breads, made rich and yellow with butter and eggs. This enrichment gives it a close texture, more like a cake than a bread. It is usually eaten at afternoon tea as a cake or at breakfast, but when sliced and toasted also forms the classic accompaniment to a foie gras terrine.

Some brioche recipes are very rich, with equal parts flour and butter, but using half the weight of butter to flour, as in this recipe, gives a more consistent result.

Crumpets

ILLUSTRATED ON PREVIOUS PAGES

MAKES 12 CRUMPETS

450g plain flour
1 tsp caster sugar
1 sachet fast-action yeast
350ml skimmed milk

350ml bottled spring water
1 tsp Maldon salt, ground fine
$1/2$ tsp bicarbonate of soda
sunflower oil

Sift the flour into a bowl with the sugar and yeast. Warm the milk and water to about 20°C, then use a hand whisk to beat this liquid into the flour to make a smooth batter. Cover the bowl with cling film and leave to stand at room temperature for about 2 hours. The batter will more than double in size before falling slightly.

Beat in the salt and bicarbonate of soda, then leave the batter to rest for 10 minutes while you heat a griddle or heavy-based frying pan over a low flame.

You must now judge whether your batter is the right consistency, which should be like that of unwhipped single cream. If too thick, the honeycomb of holes, which is the defining point of the crumpet, will not occur. If too thin, the batter will run from under the rings. If the cooking surface is too hot, the batter will burn before the crumpet is ready to be turned; if too cool, the crumpet will rise incompletely and be leaden. Test both batter and heat of pan by cooking a spoonful of batter before proceeding. If the batter is too thick, thin with a little water; if too thin, beat in a little more flour.

Moisten a piece of kitchen paper with oil and rub over the inside of the metal rings and the hot surface of the griddle, placing the rings on top. Put 3 tbsp of batter into each ring. Cook for 6–8 minutes, or until the surface is set and filled with holes. Turn the crumpets and rings over with a palette knife or spatula and cook for a further 2–3 minutes. The first side should be a chestnut brown, the second only barely coloured, and the crumpets about 3cm thick. Lift off the rings with a cloth. Eat at once, or leave to cool and then toast the pale side. Serve with butter and jam or honey.

sweet yeast breads

Crumpets have been an English tea-time favourite since the early seventeenth century, though they were originally made from buckwheat flour. In 1769 Elizabeth Raffald described 'crumpets made with wheat flour in a batter raised with a sourdough starter, cooked on a griddle, then toasted before an open fire.' Their popularity reached its zenith in the 1920s and '30s, when afternoon tea wouldn't have been complete without hot buttered crumpets and jam.

Crumpets are traditionally cooked on a flat griddle, though you can also use a heavy-based frying pan or a non-stick pan. Difficulties may come from using too much yeast, from having too solid a batter or from cooking at the wrong temperature. To make crumpets properly you will need some 8–9cm metal crumpet rings (or plain metal pastry cutters) to put on to the flat metal cooking surface.

Croissants

MAKES 16 CROISSANTS

1 sachet fast-action yeast

500g strong white flour + extra for sprinkling

110ml warm bottled spring water (20°C)

110ml cold milk (10°C)

20g Maldon salt, ground fine

70g caster sugar

250g unsalted butter

GLAZE

1 egg yolk

1 tbsp milk

Make a sponge: in a bowl, whisk together the yeast, 100g of the flour and the warm water. Cover the bowl with cling film and leave in a warm place for 2 hours, or until the sponge has risen by at least one-third and is clearly active, with lots of bubbles.

Put the remaining flour, the milk, salt and sugar in the bowl of a heavy-duty electric mixer and add the sponge. Switch on at the lowest speed and work with the dough hook for 2 minutes. Turn up the speed slightly and work for 6 minutes, when the dough will be soft and sticky and coming away from the sides of the bowl. Put the dough in a polythene bag and leave overnight in the fridge.

The next day, put a sheet of cling film on the table and dredge with flour. Lay the butter, which should be firm but not hard from the fridge, on top. (If too soft you will not be able to control it.) Sprinkle a little flour on to the butter and, with a rolling pin, knock it out into a rectangle about 1cm thick. Wrap with the cling film and place it in a cool part of the kitchen. (If the room is hot, return the butter to the fridge for a few minutes.)

Take the dough out of the bag and put it on a floured work surface. Knock back with the rolling pin. Scatter more flour on top of the dough and on the rolling pin, then roll out, turning frequently, into a rectangle about 1cm thick. Brush off any obvious flour, then put the unwrapped butter in the centre. Fold the edges of the dough over the butter so that they slightly overlap at the top and the butter is completely enclosed.

continued overleaf...

Scatter some more flour over the top. Rolling always away from you, roll the dough out into a long rectangle about 67 x 40cm. Fold one end in by a sixth and then the other end in by a sixth. Fold both ends over again by a sixth so that they meet in the centre. Now fold the two together, as if you are closing a book. Turn the dough so the fold is to one side. Roll it out gently away from you again into a long rectangle about the same size as before. Fold one end of the dough in by a quarter and then the other end in by a quarter so that they meet in the middle. Now fold the two together, as if you are closing a book. Seal the edges with pressure from the rolling pin. Wrap in cling film and refrigerate for 30 minutes to 1 hour.

Make a triangular template 17.5 x 17.5 x 15cm from card or rigid plastic. Roll the dough out on a floured surface to as neat a rectangle as you can, about 75cm long, 30cm across and 4mm thick. Trim to give straight edges, then cut into two pieces lengthways. Using the template, mark out and cut 8 triangles from each piece of dough.

Lay the triangles, one at a time, on the lightly floured surface with the narrow point away from you. Roll up, finishing with the point in the middle and underneath. Lay the croissants on large baking trays lined with non-stick baking parchment, leaving space round them to allow for expansion. Cover with cling film and leave in a warm place to rise until doubled in size, which should take 1–2 hours.

Preheat the oven to 200°C. For the glaze, whisk the egg yolk and milk together. Brush lightly on to the croissants, brushing from the middle outwards so the glaze does not get between the dough layers – this could cause them to stick and would impair the uniform rise. Bake in two batches in the centre of the oven for 10 minutes, when they will have expanded and started to colour. Reduce the oven setting to 150°C and bake for a further 20–25 minutes, or until risen and golden brown. Cool on a wire rack, arranging the croissants so they are not touching.

Croissants, originated in Vienna and were first made from enriched bread dough. The buttery yet feather-light puff pastry and yeast croissant, which has become the defining statement of a pastry cook's skill, is a comparatively recent French development, around 100 years ago. Making croissants is time-consuming and takes practice to get right, but as it is now difficult to buy a fine croissant, even in France, there is every reason to try. This is a much easier method than most, yet it produces an excellent, flaky result.

Croissants are best eaten still warm from the oven. Their high butter content means that they freeze well too. When ready to serve, put the frozen croissants into a very hot oven for 5 minutes, then remove to a rack and leave to stand for 5 minutes. Raw unproved croissants also freeze well; these should be thawed in the refrigerator overnight, then put to rise, covered, until doubled in size before baking.

Quick breads

'Quick' breads are distinguished by their use of baking powder, bicarbonate of soda and cream of tartar to generate the carbon dioxide which lightens and lifts the loaf instead of yeast. Bicarbonate of soda produces a crisper finish than baking powder. In our recipes we often use a mixture of the two to deliver a perfect texture.

Cornbread

SERVES 6

120ml milk
90g unsalted butter + extra for the tin
240g cornmeal
240g plain white flour
2 tsp baking powder
2 tsp bicarbonate of soda

1 tsp Maldon salt, ground fine
1 egg
120ml plain low-fat bio yoghurt or
   buttermilk
1 fresh green chilli, finely shredded
2 spring onions, thinly sliced

Preheat the oven to 180°C. Butter a 20cm round deep cake tin and line the bottom with buttered greaseproof paper.

Warm the milk in a small pan, then remove from the heat and add the butter. Leave to melt off the heat. Sift the dry ingredients into a mixing bowl. Beat the egg with the yoghurt or buttermilk and the buttery milk. Stir in the chilli and spring onions, then fold this mixture into the dry ingredients.

Pour the mixture into the prepared tin. Bake for about 25 minutes, or until the top is golden and the bread firm to the touch.

Turn out and cut into wedges while still hot.

Cornbread is the staple bread in the southern states of the USA. Traditionally it is flavoured with bacon fat, but you can substitute butter, lard or olive oil. You can stir various things into the batter to give the bread a different character – crisp pieces of bacon, for example, or fried onions, blanched sweetcorn kernels or, as here, some hot chilli and spring onions. Cornbreads are particularly good with fried and barbecued foods, like chicken and spare ribs.

Wholemeal soda bread

MAKES I LOAF

300ml buttermilk or thin plain low-fat bio yoghurt
I tbsp black treacle
220g self-raising white flour
220g plain wholemeal flour
I tbsp wheat germ
$1/2$ tsp cream of tartar
I tsp bicarbonate of soda
I tsp Maldon salt, ground fine
plain flour for dusting

Preheat the oven to 190°C. Warm the buttermilk with the black treacle in a small saucepan until the treacle melts. Combine all the dry ingredients in a mixing bowl. Pour over the milk and treacle mixture and mix well with your hands to make a dough. It should be soft but not too wet and sticky.

Shape into a ball and place on a floured baking tray. Cut a deep cross into the top of the loaf, taking the cuts all the way through to the bottom. Bake for 1 hour, or until the bread sounds hollow when tapped on the base.

An altogether gutsier loaf than white soda bread (overleaf), as the wheat germ and treacle impart a lot of flavour and moistness. It keeps a little better than white soda bread too, but is still best eaten immediately.

Soda bread is a great Irish tradition and should not be thought of as a tea cake. On the contrary, it is excellent with oysters or butter and cheese.

White soda bread

MAKES 1 LOAF

450g plain white flour + extra for dusting

1 tsp caster sugar

1 tsp Maldon salt, ground fine

1 tsp bicarbonate of soda

1 tsp cream of tartar

350ml buttermilk or thin plain low-fat bio yoghurt

Preheat the oven to 230°C. Sift the flour into a bowl with the sugar, salt, bicarbonate of soda and cream of tartar. Make a well in the centre. Pour in the buttermilk or yoghurt, mixing in with one hand and working from the side of the bowl inwards while turning the bowl with the other hand. The dough should be soft but not too wet and sticky. If it is too dry to hold, add a little more buttermilk.

As soon as it holds, turn out on to a lightly floured surface and knead briefly. Shape into a ball and set on a floured baking tray. Cut a deep cross into the top of the loaf, taking the cuts all the way through to the bottom.

Bake in the middle of the oven for 15 minutes, then lower the oven setting to 200°C. Continue to bake for 30 minutes, when the bread should sound hollow when tapped on the base.

Buttermilk was originally the slightly sour residue of milk from which most of the fat had been removed in churning to make butter, though today it is made commercially from skimmed milk. Healthfood shops and some supermarkets stock it. Buttermilk gives a rich and distinctive tang to the bread, but if you cannot find it, yoghurt can be substituted.

Glossary

active yeast Commercially produced yeast either in cultured or reconstituted dried forms. Also called brewers' yeast, it is made up of the living cells of the yeast strain *Saccharomyces cerevisiae*. When fresh, it is usually sold in small, moist, compressed cakes.

baguette Light (250g), long (75cm) French loaf baked with soft white flour (T550), which originated in Paris in the 1920s. It is characterised by a beautifully thick, crackling-crisp crust, but stales within hours.

baking powder This mixture of bicarbonate of soda and acid salts is a complete raising agent that only needs moisture to activate it. Also contains a large percentage of ground starch, which is included to absorb moisture from the air and prevent premature activation in the tin. It is used in conjunction with soft flour to make 'quick' breads.

banetton Linen-lined wicker basket, of different shapes and sizes, in which doughs are proved.

barm Raising agent containing yeasts from the froth produced during beer fermentation.

beignet Deep-fried, yeasted bread dough – either a plain doughnut or a fruit fritter.

bicarbonate of soda An alkali raising agent. When mixed with an acid, such as cream of tartar, a chemical reaction is kick-started and carbon dioxide is given off.

biga Italian version of poolish, based on the high-protein Italian '00' flour used for pasta.

bolting, boulting Successive sieving of flour to make whiter, refined flour.

bran Outer husk of wheat.

brioche Sweet yeasted bread enriched with butter and egg.

crumpet Yeast batter cooked in ring moulds on a griddle, to produce a crumpet with a dark brown base and a characteristic pale top pocked with holes.

deflate Pressing raised dough to expel the carbon dioxide trapped as bubbles by the gluten during proving.

fermentation Process during which carbon dioxide is given off. This is a result of yeasts producing alcohol as a by-product of getting chemical energy from sugars.

ficelle White loaf made as a baguette in length, but only 125g in weight, so much thinner.

focaccia Rectangular white bread with a dimpled surface, dressed liberally with olive oil and sea salt before baking. It often has rosemary leaves on top, too.

fougasse Provençal oval yeasted flat bread distinguished by slashed holes cut through in a rough herringbone or leaf-on-branch pattern. It may be plain or filled.

gluten Combination of two proteins in wheat grain, which bind together when moistened, creating thin, elastic strands. These form membranes that trap the gas, causing the dough to rise.

granary flour Wholemeal flour with a variety of seeds.

grissini Crisp bread sticks first made in Turin.

hard flour White wheat flour with 10–14 per cent protein.

knead Working and mixing flour and water together to make a coherent, elastic and pliable dough. Kneading can either be by hand or using an electric mixer fitted with a dough hook. It encourages the gluten in flour to stretch, expand and acquire the necessary elastic properties to trap gas bubbles given off during yeast fermentation (leavening, proving).

knock back Aggressive action to deflate dough after initial proving.

levain, leaven Dough colonised by airborne yeasts, which is used to raise sourdough breads.

meal Coarse flour.

miche Large, round French country loaf, usually a sourdough.

oats Coarse cereal eaten in porridge, muesli and oat cakes.

organic Implies something is free of chemicals or other additives and has been grown or raised in a chemical-free environment.

pane bianco Classic Italian loaf with minor regional variations throughout Italy – their version of a French pain de campagne.

peel Flat beechwood head attached to a long shaft, used for loading and unloading breads from traditional ovens.

polenta Meal ground from dried field corn (maize).

poolish Starter batter colonised by airborne yeasts, which is used to raise sourdough breads.

pretzel Loosely twisted knot of crisp white yeasted dough.

Pretzels are seen as American, though they can be traced back to Roman times.

prove To rest kneaded dough in a warm place, during which time it rises.

quick bread Bread raised using chemical raising agents, such as cornbread, soda bread, muffins and scones.

rye Low-gluten cereal. When milled it produces a dark, heavy flour with a pronounced flavour.

semolina Durum wheat that is more coarsely ground than standard wheat flours.

soda bread Soft wheat flour loaf that is typically raised with bicarbonate of soda, originating from Ireland.

soft flour White wheat flour with a protein content of between 6 and 10 per cent.

sourdough Bread leavened using wild yeasts and given a distinctive sour tang from the lengthy fermentation involved.

sponge Preliminary flour, yeast and water batter. Once active, the sponge is used to raise the subsequent dough.

spring water Purified bottled still water without added chemicals.

sumak Red powder made from the dried berries of the shrub of the same name, which is used extensively in Iraqi cooking.

taux des cendres French designation of the level of bran in a flour, based on the ash that is left behind after the flour has been incinerated in a laboratory at 900°C.

wheat germ Oily embryo of the wheat 'berry' or kernel. Wheat germ is a concentrated source of proteins, vitamins and minerals.

wholemeal, wholewheat Flours that are darker in colour because they are made using elements of the whole wheat berry including some of the wheat germ and bran.

yeast Microscopic single-cell organism that produces alcohol and carbon dioxide as it grows, a process called fermentation. To do this it needs sugars, moisture and warmth.

zatar Mixture of equal amounts of powdered sumak and dried ground marjoram and thyme.

Index

Page numbers in *italic* refer to the illustrations

A
apple juice
  rye starter, 67
  San Francisco sourdough
    starter, 64
apples
  Bramley apple sourdough,
    80–1, 84–5
apricots
  hot cross buns, *131*, 132–3

B
baguettes, 21, 22
  flour, 97
  pain blanc, 96–8, *99*
  shaping, 46–7, *46–7*
Baker & Spice, 7–13
bakers' yeast, 89
baking powder, 146
  cornbread, *148*, 149
barm, 58
bâtons, shaping, 48–9, *49*
beer froth, wild yeasts, 58–61
bicarbonate of soda, 146
  cornbread, *148*, 149
  white soda bread, 152
  wholemeal soda bread, 150,
    151
biga acida, 66
  pagnotta, 74–5

potato and rosemary bread,
  86–7, *87*
Bramley apple sourdough, *80–1*,
  84–5
bran, 18, 20, 21
bread sticks *127*, 128–9
breadcrumbs, 101
brewers' yeast, 58, 89
brioche, *134–5*, 136–7
buns, hot cross, *131*, 132–3
butter
  brioche, *134–5*, 136–7
  croissants, 142–5, *143*
buttermilk
  cornbread, *148*, 149
  white soda bread, 152
  wholemeal soda bread, 150,
    151

C
Canadian flours, 21
candied peel
  hot cross buns, *131*, 132–3
carbon dioxide
  fermentation, 58
  quick breads, 146
carta musica, 114
Celts, 58
cheese
  Roquefort and walnut fougasse,
    122, 124–5
cornbread, *148*, 149
cream of tartar, 146

white soda bread, 152
  wholemeal soda bread, 150, *151*
croissants, 142–5, *143*
crumpets, *138–9*, 140–1
crust, steam ovens, 17
currants
  rye starter, 67

D
Dan's garlic bread, 108–13,
  110–13
dough, 29–55
  handling, 31–43
  kneading, 38–40, *39–43*
  mixing soft dough, 32–7, *33–7*
  shaping loaves, 44–7, *45–9*, 49
  shaping rolls, 51–5, *52–5*
dried fruit
  hot cross buns, *131*, 132–3
  rye starter, 67
dried yeast, 89, 90

E
eggs, 25
  brioche, *134–5*, 136–7
Egypt, ancient, 58
English granary and sunflower
  seed bread, *103*, 104–5
equipment, 26–7

F
fermentation
  levain, 71

wild yeast starters, 63
wild yeasts, 58, 61
flat breads, 114–29
  focaccia, *115*, 116–17
  roast pepper and paprika bread,
    118, 119–21, *122–3*
  Roquefort and walnut fougasse,
    122, 124–5
  yeast, 114
flour, 12, 18–23
  additives, 21
  for baguettes, 97
  milling, 20–1
  T numbers, 22
  types of, 21–3
focaccia, *115*, 116–17
fougasse, Roquefort and walnut,
  122, 124–5
France
  croissants, 142–5, *143*
  flour mills, 21
  flours, 21, 22
  French wheaten rye, 100–1,
    102
  Jason's basic French levain,
    70–1, *71*
  pain au levain, 58, *80–1*, 82–3
  pain blanc, 51, 96–8, *99*
  Roquefort and walnut fougasse,
    122, 124–5
  semolina-crust pain de mie,
    106–7, *107*
  sourdough loaves, 58

G
garlic bread, Dan's, 108–13,
  110–13
gas, fermentation, 58
gas ovens, 26
Germany, rye bread, 68
gluten
  fermentation and, 58
  flour milling, 20, 21
granary flour
  English granary and sunflower
    seed bread, *103*, 104–5
  Roquefort and walnut fougasse,
    122, 124–5
grapes
  San Francisco sourdough
    starter, 64
grinding flours, 20
grissini, *127*, 128–9

H
hot cross buns, *131*, 132–3

I
improvers, 21
Italy
  focaccia, *115*, 116–17
  pagnotta, 58, 74–5
  rye bread, 68

J
Jason's basic French levain, 70–1,
  71

K
kneading dough, 38–40, *39–43*
Komarovsky, Erez, 87

L
levain, 61
  Jason's basic French levain,
    70–1, *71*
loaves, shaping, *44–7*, 45–9,
  49
long rolls, shaping, 54–5, *54–5*

M
milk
  semolina-crust pain de mie,
    106–7, *107*
milling flours, 20–1

O
oil, mixing dough, 34
orange juice
  biga acida, 66
  Dan's garlic bread, 108–13,
    110–13
  Jason's basic French levain,
    70–1, *71*
  organic wholemeal bread, *92–3*,
    94–5
  pain au levain, *80–1*, 82–3
organic wholemeal bread, *92–3*,
  94–5
oven thermometers, 26
ovens, 10, 17, 26

P

pagnotta, 58, 74–5
  grissini, *127*, 128–9
  pretzels, 126, *127*
pain au levain, 58, *80–1*, 82–3
pain blanc, 51, 96–8, *99*
pain de mie, semolina-crust,
  106–7, *107*
paprika
  roast pepper and paprika bread,
  118, 119–21, 122–3
Pasteur, Louis, 58
peppers
  roast pepper and paprika bread,
  118, 119–21, 122–3
pimenton, 121
pizzas, 117
Poland, rye bread, 61, 68
poolish, 61
  rye starter, 67–8
  San Francisco sourdough
  starter, 64–5
potato and rosemary bread, 86–7,
  87
pretzels, 126, *127*
proteins, gluten, 58

Q

quick breads, 146–52
  cornbread, 149
  white soda bread, 152
  wholemeal soda bread, 150,
  151

R

Raffald, Elizabeth, 141
raisins
  hot cross buns, *131*, 132–3
refreshing starters, 64–5
roast pepper and paprika bread,
  118, 119–21, *122–3*
roller milling, 20
rolls, shaping, 51–5, *52–5*
Romans, 58
room temperature, 24
Roquefort and walnut fougasse,
  122, 124–5
rosemary
  focaccia, *115*, 116–17
  potato and rosemary bread,
  86–7, 87
round loaves, shaping, *44–5*, 45
round rolls, shaping, 52–3, *52–3*
rye bread, 58, 68
  French wheaten rye, 100–1,
  102
rye flour, 23
rye starter, 67–8
  Bramley apple sourdough,
  80–1, 84–5
  French wheaten rye, 100–1, *102*

S

Saccharomyces cerevisiae, 89
salt, 25
San Francisco sourdough, *76–7*,
  78–9

San Francisco sourdough starter,
  64–5
self-raising flour, 18, 21
  wholemeal soda bread, *150*,
  151
semolina-crust pain de mie,
  106–7, *107*
shaped breads, 114–29
  grissini, *127*, 128–9
  pretzels, 126, *127*
shaping loaves, 44–7, *45–9*, 49
shaping rolls, 51–5, *52–5*
soda bread
  white soda bread, 152
  wholemeal soda bread, 150,
  151
soft dough, 32–7, *33–7*
sourdough, 16–17, 58–61
  Bramley apple sourdough,
  80–1, 84–5
  San Francisco sourdough,
  76–7, 78–9
  San Francisco sourdough
  starter, 64–5
  wild yeast starters, 57, 58, 61
starters
  biga acida, 66
  Jason's basic French levain,
  70–1, *71*
  refreshing, 64–5
  rye starter, 67–8
  San Francisco sourdough
  starter, 64–5

wild yeast starters, 57–71

steam ovens, 17

stoneground flours, 20–1, 22

sunflower seeds

  English granary and sunflower
    seed bread, *103*, 104–5

  Roquefort and walnut fougasse,
    122, 124–5

sweet yeast breads, 130–45

  brioche, *134–5*, 136–7

  croissants, 142–5, *143*

  crumpets, *138–9*, 140–1

  hot cross buns, *131*, 132–3

T

temperature

  room, 24

  sourdough starters, 61

  water, 24

testing loaves, 25

thermometers, oven, 26

tortillas, 114

V

Vienna, 145

W

walnuts

  Roquefort and walnut fougasse,
    122, 124–5

water, 25

  temperature, 24

wheat flour, 18–20

wheat germ, 20, 21

  pain au levain, *80–1*, 82–3

  wholemeal soda bread, 150,
    151

wheaten rye, French, 100–1, *102*

white soda bread, 152

wholemeal bread, organic, *92–3*,
  94–5

wholemeal flour, 21, 23

wholemeal loaves, 19

wholemeal soda bread, 150, *151*

wholeweat flour, 21

Y

yeast, 24

  commercial yeasts, 89–113

  dried yeast, 89, 90

  flat breads, 114

  fresh yeast, 89

  sweet yeast breads, 130–45

  wild yeast breads, 73–87

  wild yeast starters, 12, 13,
    57–71

yoghurt

  cornbread, *148*, 149

  rye starter, 67

  San Francisco sourdough
    starter, 64–5

  white soda bread, 152

  wholemeal soda bread, 150, *151*

Acknowledgements

Baker & Spice
47 Denyer Street
London SW3 2LX

020 7589 4734

www.bakerandspice.com

We have many full-time staff working to create the food we make every day. Of course, they change from time to time, but without the extreme hard work and dedication of our exceptional crew we would not be where we are today. Staff who have helped to create the shop we have today, listed chronologically, are:

For the bakery: David Frequelin, Remi Georgelin, DL, Amir Allon, Martin Aspinwall, Jason Warwick, Remek Sanetra, Henri Bellon de Chassy, Damon Cowan, Sally Parsons, Amar Slimani.

For the Viennoiserie: Patrick Lozach, Ram Sivaram, Martin Doak, Lionel Rocher, Ilan Schwartz, Mariangela Pratt.

For the pâtisserie: Henri Berthaud, Yannick, Amal Ibrahim, Ari Aboso, Alexandra Queruel, Yvan Cahour, Dorit Meinzer, Jeanne Hertz, Linda Osedo, Louise Riviere, Jaime Foa, Megan Jones, Mark Lazenby, Markus Herz, James Webb.

For the traiteur: Lorraine Dunne, Sammy Leopold Santos, DL, Michelle Wong, Kate Lewis, Sami Tamimi, Ruth Taylor Hunt, Pavel Kuzdak, Cayetano Lopez.

For the shop: Karen Copland, Natalie Laurent, Zoe Field, Tamsin Borlase, Anne Boyle, Fiona Kinnear, Stephane Boucton, Leonor Gomez, Laurent Beauvois, Helena Allon, Fabio Calascibetta, Alessandra Figini, Belen Mateo, Jaclyn Dove, Emma O'Reilly, Naima Ali, Anna Plym, Jenny Mellquist, Andrea Novak, Eric Ackermann, Daniel Marcolin, David Doulay, Candice Nieper, Kirsty McGregor, Amanda Hale, Anna-Marie Briers, Ari Economakis.

Kitchen assistants: Vince Mejia, Tito Bosales, Cesar Aristizabal.

For the bread factory and gail force: Amnon Mer, Pierre Corneille, Richard Vintiner, Samantha Oyez, Jackie Hobbs, Terry Stockwell, Nimal Kandihi.

Our drivers: David Ormston, Paul Stimson, Steve Bragg, Richard Fenton, Ray Mechell, Errol Palmer, Arthur Albert.

Our friends: Melanie Pini and Sophie Braimbridge (who suggested and created our first series of chef demonstrations), Naomi Kaplan (forever a source of inspiration), Anissa Helou, Peter Gordon, Jeremy Lee, Lyn Hall, Ursula Ferrigno, Giorgio Locatelli, Elizabeth Luard, Alastair Little, Juliet Peston, Heston Blumenthal, Jonathan Archer, John Kelly, Enzo Zaccharini, Honor Chapman, Sarah Standing, and all those customers who have supported us from the beginning.

All our recipes have an origin, as do the recipes in every cookbook. Though these recipes have been written or adapted and tested especially by Dan Lepard and Richard Whittington, the inspiration has come from friends. We would also like to thank Jason Warwick for the basic levain and Roquefort and walnut fougasse.

For the production of this book, Baker & Spice would like to thank Divertimenti of Fulham, Kitchen Aid UK, Phillip Brittain and Solstice, Neal's Yard Dairy, Jeni Wright, Peter Howard, Coralie Bickford-Smith, Bridget Bodoano and Caroline Perkins.

We would like to thank Emily Andersen for the use of her photographs on pages 7 (centre), 9, 12, 14–15, 26, 28–9, 41, 57 (centre), 89 (centre), 91 and 153.

Baker & Spice breads are available through Neal's Yard Dairy, mail order in UK mainland only (020 7407 1800).

If you find you have difficulty obtaining any item of kitchen equipment, then Nisbets of Bath offer a mail order service (01454 855555).